PROCEEDINGS
OF THE

EIGHTH WORLD CONFERENCE on EARTHQUAKE ENGINEERING

July 21-28, 1984
San Francisco
California
U.S.A.

PROCEEDINGS

OF THE

EIGHTH WORLD CONFERENCE on EARTHQUAKE ENGINEERING

July 21–28, 1984
San Francisco
California
U.S.A.

POST-CONFERENCE VOLUME

Prentice-Hall, Englewood Cliffs, New Jersey 07632

Library of Congress Catalog Card Number: 57-27345

ISBN 0-13-722901-1   01

Prentice-Hall International, Inc., *London*
Prentice-Hall of Australia Pty. Limited, *Sidney*
Editora Prentice-Hall do Brasil, Ltda., *Rio de Janeiro*
Prentice-Hall Canada Inc., *Toronto*
Prentice-Hall of India Private Limited, *New Delhi*
Prentice-Hall of Japan, Inc., *Tokyo*
Prentice-Hall of Southeast Asia Pte. Ltd., *Singapore*
Whitehall Books Limited, *Wellington, New Zealand*

SPONSORING ORGANIZATION:
*International Association
for Earthquake Engineering*

HOST ORGANIZATION:
Earthquake Engineering Research Institute

in cooperation with:
*American Concrete Institute
American Geophysical Union
American Institute of Architects
American Nuclear Society
American Society of Civil Engineers
American Society of Mechanical Engineers
Applied Technology Council
Association of Engineering Geologists
Building Seismic Safety Council
Seismological Society of America
Structural Engineers Association of California*

SPONSORING ORGANIZATION

International Association
for Earthquake Engineering (IAEE)

KENCHIKU KAIKAN 3rd Floor
5-26-20, Shiba, Minato-ku
Tokyo 108, Japan

Cable Address: INTERQUAKE TOKYO

President: Donald E. Hudson
Executive Vice-President: Hajime Umemura
Vice-President: Joseph Penzien
Secretary General: Yutaka Osawa
Directors: A.S. Arya (India)
T. Boen (Indonesia)
J. Carmona (Argentina)
N.O. Henaku (Ghana)
A.O. Hizon (Philippines)
K. Kubo (Japan)
J. Kuroiwa (Peru)
A.I. Martemianov (USSR)
J. Petrovski (Yugoslavia)
J. Prince (Mexico)
R.I. Skinner (New Zealand)

The International Association for Earthquake Engineering brings together national organizations from 34 countries with the object of promoting international cooperation among scientists and engineers through interchange of knowledge, ideas, and the results of research and practical experience. In addition to the principal activity of sponsoring the World Conferences on Earthquake Engineering at 4-year intervals, IAEE publishes regularly the book *Earthquake Resistant Regulations—a World List,* has issued a special monograph on "Basic Concepts of Seismic Codes," and sponsors such activities as the International Strong Motion Accelerograph Committee.

HOST ORGANIZATION

Earthquake Engineering
Research Institute (EERI)
2260 Telegraph Avenue
Berkeley, California 94704, U.S.A.

President: Mihran S. Agbabian
Vice-President: Richard A. Parmelee
Secretary/Treasurer: Henry J. Lagorio
Directors: M.S. Agbabian
N.M. Hawkins
W.W. Hays
H.J. Lagorio
R.A. Parmelee
F.R. Preece
J.C. Stepp
A. Stevens
R.V. Whitman

Association Director: Susan Newman
Technical Director: Roger E. Scholl

The Earthquake Engineering Research Institute is the U.S. national professional society devoted to finding better ways to protect life and property from the effects of earthquakes. Its objectives are the advancement of the science and practice of earthquake engineering and the solution of national earthquake engineering problems.

ORGANIZING COMMITTEES
8TH WORLD CONFERENCE ON EARTHQUAKE ENGINEERING
SAN FRANCISCO, CALIFORNIA
JULY 1984

STEERING COMMITTEE

Joseph Penzien, Chair
University of California, Berkeley

Mihran S. Agbabian (Ex-Officio)
Agbabian Associates, El Segundo, California

Anil K. Chopra
University of California, Berkeley

Neville C. Donovan
Dames & Moore, San Francisco

Paul C. Jennings
California Institute of Technology, Pasadena

Roy G. Johnston
Brandow & Johnston Associates, Los Angeles

Christopher Rojahn
Applied Technology Council, Palo Alto, California

Haresh C. Shah
Stanford University, Stanford, California

Beverly Wyllie
Lafayette, California

Loring A. Wyllie, Jr.
H.J. Degenkolb & Associates, San Francisco

ARRANGEMENTS COMMITTEE

Neville C. Donovan, Chair
Dames & Moore, San Francisco

Ann M. Becker
Dames & Moore, San Francisco

Charles F. Knudson
Lafayette, California

Otto W. Steinhardt
Pacific Gas & Electric Company, San Francisco

Mary Ann Wagner
H.J. Degenkolb & Associates, San Francisco

FINANCE COMMITTEE

Roy G. Johnston, Chair
Brandow & Johnston Associates, Los Angeles

Mihran S. Agbabian
Agbabian Associates, El Segundo, California

John A. Blume
URS/J.A. Blume & Associates, San Francisco

L. LeRoy Crandall
LeRoy Crandall & Associates, Los Angeles

Henry J. Degenkolb
H.J. Degenkolb & Associates, San Francisco

George W. Housner
California Institute of Technology, Pasadena

William W. Moore
Dames & Moore, San Francisco

BUDGET COMMITTEE

Anil K. Chopra, Chair
University of California, Berkeley

Roy G. Johnston
Brandow & Johnston Associates, Los Angeles

Susan Newman
Earthquake Engineering Research Institute,
Berkeley, California

Haresh C. Shah
Stanford University, Stanford, California

Charles C. Thiel
Piedmont, California

INFORMATION COMMITTEE

Christopher Rojahn, Chair
Applied Technology Council, Palo Alto, California

A. Gerald Brady
U.S. Geological Survey, Menlo Park, California

Lloyd S. Cluff
Woodward Clyde Consultants, Walnut Creek, California

Eric Elsesser
Forell/Elsesser Engineers, San Francisco

Mary W. Henderson
Redwood City, California

Henry J. Lagorio
University of California, Berkeley

Thomas V. McEvilly
University of California, Berkeley

PROCEEDINGS COMMITTEE

Haresh C. Shah, Chair
  Stanford University, Stanford, California
Nicholas B. Forell
  Forell/Elsesser Engineers, San Francisco
Jeremy Isenberg
  Weidlinger Associates, Menlo Park, California
Charles C. Kircher
  J.R. Benjamin Associates, Mountain View, California
George G. Mader
  William Spangle & Associates, Portola Valley, California
Martin W. McCann
  J.R. Benjamin Associates, Mountain View, California
T. Leslie Youd
  U.S. Geological Survey, Menlo Park, California
Theodore C. Zsutty
  San Jose State University, San Jose, California

PROGRAM COMMITTEE

Paul C. Jennings, Chair
  California Institute of Technology, Pasadena
Neville C. Donovan
  Dames & Moore, San Francisco
Ray W. Clough
  University of California, Berkeley
Asadour H. Hadjian
  Bechtel Power Corporation, Los Angeles
William J. Hall
  University of Illinois, Urbana
Helmut Krawinkler
  Stanford University, Stanford, California
Robert A. Olson
  VSP Associates, Sacramento, California
Clarkson W. Pinkham
  S.B. Barnes & Associates, Los Angeles
Lawrence G. Selna
  University of California, Los Angeles
Robin Shepherd
  University of California, Irvine
Charles C. Thiel
  Piedmont, California
Robert E. Wallace
  U.S. Geological Survey, Menlo Park, California
Robert V. Whitman
  Massachusetts Institute of Technology, Cambridge

SPECIAL EVENTS COMMITTEE

Beverly Wyllie, Co-Chair
  Lafayette, California
Loring A. Wyllie, Jr, Co-Chair
  H.J. Degenkolb & Associates, San Francisco
Robert Burford
  U.S. Geological Survey, Menlo Park, California
Ted and Jan Cannon
  Greenbrae, California
James and Janice Gere
  Stanford, California
William and Ursula Holmes
  Oakland, California
Robert and Beth Janopaul
  Atherton, California
Donald and Carol Javete
  Oakland, California
Robert and Bebe Lawson
  Greenbrae, California
Stephen A. Mahin
  University of California, Berkeley
Hugh D. McNiven
  University of California, Berkeley
Robert and Ann Preece
  San Francisco, California

ACCOMPANYING PERSONS PROGRAM SUBCOMMITTEE

Carol Forell, Chair
  Tiburon, California
Anna Degenkolb
  San Francisco, California
Judie Donovan
  San Rafael, California
Sylvia Elsesser
  Sausalito, California
Janice Gere
  Stanford, California
Michele Krawinkler
  Los Altos, California
Natalie Lagorio
  Orinda, California
Jeanne Penzien
  Lafayette, California
Irene Popov
  Berkeley, California
Ann Preece
  San Francisco, California
Jo Rinne
  Kensington, California
Joan Shah
  Stanford, California
Lois Shapiro
  San Francisco, California
Jane Sharpe
  Los Altos, California
Betty Steinbrugge
  El Cerrito, California
Ellen Thiel
  Piedmont, California

PREFACE

The world conferences on earthquake engineering, which are held every four years under the sponsorship of the International Association of Earthquake Engineering (IAEE), had their beginning with the World Conference on Earthquake Engineering held in Berkeley, California, in 1956 to commemorate the 50th anniversary of the 1906 San Francisco earthquake. At the follow-up Second World Conference on Earthquake Engineering (2WCEE) in Tokyo-Kyoto, Japan, in 1960, the IAEE was officially formed, and the precedent was set to hold the world conferences on earthquake engineering every four years under its sponsorship. Since the 2WCEE, the conferences have been held in Auckland-Wellington, New Zealand, in 1965; Santiago, Chile, in 1969; Rome, Italy, in 1973; New Delhi, India, in 1977; and in Istanbul, Turkey, in 1980.

Interest in the world conferences has steadily increased as evidenced by the growth in the size of the conference proceedings and the number of participating countries. The 1956 Berkeley Conference proceedings consist of a single volume containing 40 papers from 12 different countries. In contrast, the 8WCEE proceedings consist of seven volumes containing approximately 800 papers from 54 countries and one Post-Conference Volume. The scope of the conferences has also broadened as reflected by the following topic areas covered in the proceedings:

- Seismic risk and hazard.
- Ground motion and seismicity.
- Soil stability, soil-structure interaction, and foundations.
- Experimental methods and tests of structures and components.
- Design of structures and structural components.
- Special structures and critical facilities.
- Response of structures.
- Repair, strengthening, and retrofit of structures.
- Urban design, socioeconomic issues, and public policy.
- Lifelines—utility and transportation systems.
- Non-structural systems and building contents.
- Development and enforcement of seismic codes and standards.

This Post-Conference Volume includes the proceedings of the Opening and Closing Ceremonies, the Keynote Address and the Conference Lecture, the Luncheon Addresses, the Statutes of the IAEE, Minutes of Meetings, the IAEE Executive Committee Membership List, the National Delegates List, and the List of Attendees at the 8WCEE.

We commend the authors of the papers included in the Proceedings for their important contributions, as the information they provide will contribute significantly to our common goal, which is to mitigate loss of life and property damage due to future earthquakes.

The Steering Committee,
8WCEE

CONTENTS

PROCEEDINGS
OF THE

EIGHTH WORLD CONFERENCE on EARTHQUAKE ENGINEERING

July 21-28, 1984
San Francisco
California
U.S.A.

I. OPENING CEREMONIES

Dr. Joseph Penzien presiding

July 23, 1984

I should like to introduce myself. I am Joe Penzien, Professor of Structural Engineering at the University of California, Berkeley. It has been my privilege and pleasure to serve as Chairman of the Steering Committee of this the Eighth World Conference on Earthquake Engineering (8WCEE) which I now declare open.

INTRODUCTORY REMARKS BY 8WCEE STEERING COMMITTEE CHAIRMAN, DR. JOSEPH PENZIEN

Distinguished Guests, Officers and Delegates of the International Association of Earthquake Engineering, Ladies and Gentlemen:

It is indeed a pleasure for me to welcome all of you to these Opening Ceremonies of the Eighth World Conference on Earthquake Engineering, especially those of you who have traveled from far distant places to be here.

Our technical participant registration now exceeds 1500 with 54 different countries being represented from around the world. Those of you from the United States would be interested to know that 40 of our 50 states are represented. Considering this large attendance with its wide geographical representation and the approximate 800 technical papers which will be presented, I am confident this Conference will be highly successful.

It is fitting that the Conference be held here in San Francisco, a city that mother nature has blessed with its beautiful surroundings and good climate -- yet, a city that must continually face the threat of one of nature's greatest hazards - earthquakes. The city is located just a few miles from the eastern edge of the Pacific plate which is delineated along the California coast by the San Andreas fault.

Considering the approximate two inches of north-south relative displacement taking place across the fault each year, the city will certainly experience a large earthquake sometime in the future causing major property damage, loss of lives, and personal injuries.

The picture on the cover of your FINAL PROGRAM, showing the city in ruins following the 1906 Earthquake and Fire, is a reminder of the danger we face.

It may be comforting however for you to know that the Fairmont Hotel building, where most of our Conference activities are being held, is the same structure shown in the cover picture. It survived the 1906 Earthquake with little structural damage.

You should not worry about the presence of the scaffolding now surrounding the hotel building. It is there simply to allow some corrective measures to be taken to improve the seismic resistance of the parapets at roof level.

The technical papers to be presented this week cover a variety of topics in the general areas of engineering seismology, structural engineering, geotechnical engineering, public policy, preparedness, and planning.

These papers will be presented in one of two formats: (1) the traditional formal oral presentation, or (2) a poster type display presentation with informal discussion. I hope all of you will find it possible to attend both types of presentations.

We are extremely fortunate to have so many outstanding papers being presented during the Conference this week, as much is to be learned regarding the effects of earthquakes and how to cope with them. These papers provide an excellent overview of earthquake engineering research and practice throughout the world.

In addition to attending the technical sessions, I trust each of you will take advantage of the opportunity this Conference provides to informally exchange views on topics of mutual interest with other specialists, for we all share a common goal, which is the mitigation of loss of life, personal injury, and property damage during future earthquakes.

Thank you.

Penzien – The Host Organization for our Conference is the Earthquake Engineering Research Institute (EERI). It is now my pleasure to introduce its President, Dr. Mihran S. Agbabian.

WELCOMING REMARKS

M. S. AGBABIAN
PRESIDENT, EERI

Twenty-eight years after the First World Conference on Earthquake Engineering was held across the Bay in Berkeley, we are here in San Francisco at the opening ceremony of the Eighth World Conference on Earthquake Engineering. Our technical community of engineers and scientists gathers every four years to present our findings and to exchange ideas and knowledge on how to mitigate the hazards of earthquakes, how to plan and prepare for future earthquakes, and how to recover from disastrous earthquakes. Significant progress has been made in all these areas. Experimental and analytical studies, surveys, measurements, and innovative ideas in design and construction have contributed to this progress. This effort has, to a large extent, identified the sources of the hazard and methods of reducing death and injury and preventing catastrophic damage to property. Unfortunately, this dedicated effort of engineers and scientists can only reduce but cannot eliminate the hazard.

It has been said, "earthquakes don't kill people, buildings do." There are more buildings in moderate to high seismic areas that were constructed without any attention to principles of earthquake resistance than there are buildings that were designed in accordance with codes and regulations that provide some level of earthquake resistance.

During the years spanning the period between the first and eighth World Conferences – from 1956 to 1984 – 57 earthquakes have caused death and major destruction: 6 at magnitude 8.0 or over, and 34 at magnitudes between 7.0 and 8.0. A total of 447,400 deaths have been reported, equal

to approximately half the population of the city of San Francisco. We don't know how much higher this death toll would have been if earthquake resistance provisions had not been incorporated in some of the locations where these earthquakes occurred. But we can feel confident that our efforts have brought some degree of safety and comfort to people around the world, and that our future efforts - some of which may be inspired by this conference - will produce even greater safety in all the seismic regions of the world.

Every four years we talk to each other in the language of scientists and engineers, enthusiastic about our new discoveries and new ideas. The World Conference acts as a forum for these technical exchanges. But it is more than that. It is a catalyst that brings us together from many countries to consolidate our work for the welfare of mankind. We represent more than forty countries concerned with the humanitarian goal of saving lives.

On behalf of the Earthquake Engineering Research Institute, and all engineers and scientists in the United States who believe in the importance of our work, I welcome you all to the Eighth World Conference on Earthquake Engineering. I am confident that the conference will be productive, old friendships will be renewed, and new friendships will be created. I hope your stay in San Francisco will be pleasant and enjoyable, and when you return to your homes you will remember that you are a member of a world team dedicated to a noble task. Let us hope that four years from now, we all will meet again at the Ninth World Conference on Earthquake Engineerng.

Today it is my privilege and pleasure to welcome you to the Eighth World Conference on Earthquake Engineering.

Penzien - As all of you know, the Sponsoring Organization for our Conference is the International Association for Earthquake Engineering (IAEE). I now have the pleasure of introducing its President, Dr. Donald E. Hudson.

WELCOMING REMARKS

D. E. HUDSON
PRESIDENT, IAEE

Professor Penzien and members of the Steering Committee for the Eighth World Conference; Dr. Agbabian; National Delegates and Officers of the International Association; distinguished guests, fellow participants, ladies and gentlemen:

I have the privilege and pleasure of extending to you all a warm welcome to this Conference on behalf of the sponsoring organization, the International Association for Earthquake Engineering. I should like to express the appreciation of our Association to our host, the Earthquake Engineering Research Institute, for the invitation to hold our Eighth World Conference here in San Francisco, and for the long years of careful preparation they have devoted to this event, which is by far the largest World Conference to date. We are returned to the San Francisco area 28 years after the First World Conference in Berkeley, having had in the meantime very successful meetings in Japan, New Zealand, Chile, Italy, India, and Turkey. These periodic Conferences have all been important milestones in the development of our relatively young field, and there is every indication that our present meeting will play an equally important role in consolidating past accomplishments and in laying the foundation for future developments.

As earthquake engineers, our goal is to prevent earthquakes from becoming disasters - to free mankind from the ever-present threat of destructive earthquakes. Our task is far from finished - since the last World Conference in Istanbul in 1980, about 15,000 persons have lost their lives in earthquake disasters, in 23 different countries. That this toll is somewhat less than the average of some 15,000 earthquake deaths per year for this century is largely fortuitous, depending on the timing and location of the earthquakes. As in the past, practically all of this death toll is the consequence of collapse of dwellings, mostly of a type well known to be little resistant to earthquake shocks. This

9

points up the major goal for us all – how to solve the economic and social problems which condemn so large a fraction of the world's population to live in structures which offer so little protection against these inevitable events.

It is to this goal that our International Association for Earthquake Engineering is dedicated. We bring together representatives of the earthquake engineering organizations from 34 countries, with new countries being added each year as the world realizes more and more the dimensions of the earthquake problem. By the sponsorship of the World Conference, by participation in related national and international meetings, by the publication of monographs on earthquake-resistant design, and through the efforts of committees addressing specific technical problems, we hope to make steady progress towards our goal.

I am sure that the interchange of ideas during the next few days will help us all to clarify our thoughts, and will inspire us to press onward even more diligently to our goal of freeing mankind from the earthquake hazard.

I should like to again thank our hosts, all of you for your participation, and to wish everyone a very successful Conference.

Thank you.

Penzien – I should now like to introduce the other gentlemen present with me here on stage. We are indeed fortunate to have all 5 past presidents of IAEE present with us here today, namely Dr. George Housner, Dr. Jai Krishna, the first and founding president Dr. Kiyoshi Muto, Mr. John Rinne, and Dr. Emilio Rosenblueth. Also with us is the Executive Vice-President of IAEE Dr. Hajime Umemura and its Secretary General Dr. Yutaka Osawa.

I now have the great honor to introduce our keynote speaker Dr. Frank Press.

Dr. Press received his undergraduate degree in physics from the City College of New York, and his advanced degrees from Columbia University in 1946 and 1949 when he joined the Columbia University faculty working in the areas of geophysics and oceanography.

In 1955, he was appointed Professor of Geophysics at the California Institute of Technology, and two years later became Director of its Seismological Laboratory.

In 1965, he was named head of the then Department of Geology and Geophysics at the Massachusetts Institute of Technology (MIT), which under his leadership, expanded into planetary sciences, oceanography, interdisciplinary studies, and a joint program with the Woods Hole Oceanographic Institution, and was renamed the Department of Earth and Planetary Sciences.

In 1977, he was appointed by President Carter as the President's Science Advisor and Director of the Office of Science and Technology Policy.

In January 1981, he returned to MIT where he was appointed Institute Professor, a title MIT reserves for scholars of special distinction.

Dr. Press returned to Washington in July 1981 as the 19th President of the National Academy of Sciences.

Dr. Press is recognized internationally for his pioneering contributions to geophysics, oceanography, lunar and planetary sciences and natural resource exploration, but his primary scientific activities have been in seismology and the study of the earth's deep interior.

He is a member of several professional organizations, and is a former President of both the Seismological Society of America and the American Geophysical Union. He was elected to the National Academy of Sciences in 1958, the American Academy of Arts and Sciences in 1966, and the American Philosophical Society.

In 1981 he was elected as foreign member of the French Academy of Sciences, and to the Board of Trustees, of both the Sloan Foundation and Rockefeller University, as well as to membership in the Corporation of MIT.

He is the recipient of numerous honors -- a list that is much too long to enumerate at this time.

His unique distinction lies perhaps in the dual contribution of the impact of his scientific work on the development of modern geophysics and the influence of his personal leadership in national science planning and administration.

It is indeed my pleasure to now introduce Dr. Frank Press who will speak on the subject "The Role of Science and Engineering in Mitigating Natural Hazards".

KEYNOTE ADDRESS: THE ROLE OF SCIENCE AND ENGINEERING IN MITIGATING NATURAL HAZARDS

BY

DR. FRANK PRESS, PRESIDENT, U.S. NATIONAL ACADEMY OF SCIENCES

Dr. Penzien, President Hudson, President Agbabian, Delegates, Fellow Scientists and Engineers. This is the second Keynote Address in San Francisco in a week. The first dealt with a political approach to assure the well being and security of people. This one has the same goal -- using the tools of science and engineering. And both are needed if we are to address many of the global problems that we all face. It is a pleasure and an honor for me to participate in the Eighth World Conference on Earthquake Engineering for several reasons. The study of earthquakes is my own profession, and it is a great pleasure to renew the relationships I've had over the years with so many colleagues.

This gathering of some 1500 leading researchers and practitioners from 50 countries is a signal event, with a superb program which gives evidence of the tremendous progress in this key field, progress that will lend impetus to a worldwide attack on the earthquake problem. And most important, there is no higher calling for a scientist and engineer than to use his talents on behalf of his fellow man. Perusing the program, one cannot but be impressed by the remarkable progress of recent years with new theoretical approaches, new data, and new kinds of experiments. And it is indeed heartening to see so many young people together with some of us who've been around for a while in this vigorous, renewing field.

I would like to organize my remarks this morning around four topics: Some generalizations about natural hazards, the role of scientists and engineers in hazard mitigation, the role of governments. And I would like to conclude with a proposal for your consideration.

A philosopher once said, "man lives by geological consent subject to change without notice". That one sentence encompasses much of the story

of life on earth. Our planet is unique in its ability to give rise to life. It's not so big as to keep by gravity a massive, crushing atmosphere, and it's not so small as to lose its atmosphere into space. It's not too far from the sun as to be cold and uninhabitable, nor is it too near. And that distance is critical by perhaps only 10 or 15 million miles. It has an internal engine fueled by radioactivity that produced the continents, the oceans, the atmosphere, and minerals, but also produces earthquakes, and volcanic eruptions. It has an external engine fueled by the sun that spreads warmth, produces rain, energy for life, but also hurricanes, floods, typhoons, tornadoes. And finally it allowed for the evolution of man, conqueror of nature, provider of food and shelter, but also destroyer, inventor of tools destruction rivaling nature. Earth is a uniquely hospitable place compared to our neighbors Venus and Mars.

But hazards come with the territory. They are rare, low probability events with consequences that are large in terms of destruction--which leads me to my first generalization. The class of hazards characterized by low probability of occurrence and high consequences presents a difficult public policy problem: how to sustain public interest and involvement; how to attract adequate government resources for mitigation programs? It's easy to understand how a country with a recent severe catastrophe, such as Tokyo in 1923 or Tangshan in 1976, can become concerned and organize national programs. But it is the height of a civilized society to anticipate and control rather than to react only after a disaster. My second generalization: Earthquakes are a special category of hazards in that most human losses are due to failure of human-made structures -- buildings, dams, lifelines, and so on. Therefore, in principle, with sufficient resources for research, development, education, followed by necessary investments in hazard reduction, earthquakes are a hazard that are within our power to respond to. We can reduce their threat over time as much as we want to. We can learn where not to build and how to build so that failure of structures will not occur. The third generalization: A comprehensive program of hazard reduction includes prediction, hazard reduction, in different ways for different kinds of hazards and in different ways for different countries. Let me give you an example: Hurricanes. The prediction of hurricanes in many countries is at a high stage of accuracy, and prediction of hurricanes saves lives. The warning is sufficient to evacuate populations from low lands and to take the necessary precautions. Hazard reduction, in the case of hurricanes, beyond prediction, consists of instituting appropriate regulations for construction, sensible insurance policies which provide disincentives for construction in flood plains and low coastal areas, education, and so on. In this way hazard reduction can reduce economic loss. Prediction of hurricanes can certainly save lives.

In the case of earthquakes, prediction is uncertain. It may only be achieved partially for certain classes of faults. It may never be achieved. Therefore, hazard reduction is key to saving lives and reducing economic loss. Prediction and hazard reduction complement each other in different ways for different kinds of hazards. And there are, of course, country differences. A typhoon in a country with poor communications and poor transportation might be predictable using global satellite means and other techniques, but it is still deadly under today's circumstances. Thus hazards vary in man's ability to predict, to control and to respond to. They vary by hazard and by country. Earthquakes represent an example of a hazard that may not be liable to prediction or control in the near term, but whose consequences can nevertheless greatly be reduced.

Let me say something about the role of scientists and engineers, and social scientists as well. The tradition of science goes back, of course, to ancient times when the fear of nature could only be dispelled by explaining nature's catastrophes. In the early days, of course, they were explained through religious myths, through astrology. And then with the advance of science came an understanding of natural phenomena, which assured people, and led to the beginnings of mitigation programs. Progress in both science and technology brings us to the present day and our ability to intervene and reduce hazards. The role of scientists and engineers are complementary, they are mutually supportive as this

16

conference shows. I am impressed at the progress since my own times as a contributor to this field, the progress manifested by scientists and engineers working together as partners, actually crossing over fields as well. Today there are scientists predicting ground motions from realistic models of faults, ground motions of the kind that are useful to engineers, taking into account transmission paths, rock types, topography. Engineers are refining magnitude scales that were originally developed by scientists. Scientists and engineers are jointly developing different kinds of risk assessment techniques. There is a blurring of fields, and this is indeed healthy. This is not to minimize the distinctive contributions of the different professions--scientists studying the nature of faulting and their possible contributions to the prediction of earthquakes; engineers, of course, in their traditional important work in the design of earthquake resistant structures; and social scientists pointing up the social and economic consequences of replacing low cost housing and commercial space which are also hazards at the same time.

A major problem for scientists and engineers, especially in the field of hazard mitigation, is to separate their role as professionals making analyses, listing options, from their political roles as citizens advocating partisan solutions. And here, I suppose, each of us has to make his own decision. I believe that we can indeed separate hazard assessment, which is essentially a technical, professional activity from hazard management, which is a political role of governments. With assessment, we evaluate risks, we analyze procedures for mitigating hazards, and we do this as professionals. This process educates the public and leads, hopefully, to informed decisions by government officials who have the responsibility for hazard management as a proper part of the political process.

Let me expand on the appropriate role for professionals in this highly charged field, for I believe the subject needs intensive discussion. There is a perception that scientists and engineers receive public funds without accounting to the public by way of explanation, by way of progress reports, the results of public support. I think this is a particular problem in your field because of the potential for hysteria, the severe human and economic consequences of a disaster, and the repression of reality in people's minds to avoid thinking about the consequences of earthquakes. I believe therefore that it is particularly important for scientists and engineers working in earthquake research to be concerned with public education—by way of lectures, articles, films, visits to communities and schools. And, of course, the key job of professionals in the earthquake field is to lay out programs appropriate to each country, involving assessment of risks, construction codes and standards, land use, criteria for the identification of safe and unsafe structures, the maintenance of lifelines during disasters and after disasters, emergency services, public education and training. Our knowledge is imperfect and therefore it is part of our job to propose a research and development program involving all aspects of the field—ground motion, soil mechanics, structural dynamics, the design of structures, the social and economic aspects, and the training of technical manpower to provide adequate back-up for this important endeavor. However, if governments do not assume their proper role of hazard management after being provided the assessment of professionals, hazard mitigation will not occur.

There are three factors which determine the destructiveness of an earthquake—its magnitude, its distance from a population center, and the degree of preparedness. A country with poor preparedness will suffer more than one with good preparedness. Good government management is the key factor in preparedness, and therefore government performance is a major controllable factor influencing the impact of a disaster. With all of the possibilities for reducing the hazards of earthquakes mentioned earlier—the codes, the land-use procedures, the emergency services, the public training, the research and development programs, the training of professionals—why do some countries have inadequate preparedness programs? Of course, there are countries that are very poor, with meager technical and financial resources, and one can understand why they would lag behind. But it is difficult to understand the short-sightedness of some advanced nations.

When I was serving in government, an official in the Office of Management and Budget once posed the following to me: "You scientists always want more. How do you know when you've had enough?" I answered in terms that he could understand. First, in financial terms involving return on research and development investments, then in human terms involving the obligation of governments to provide for the security of its people in terms of its economic growth. I also answered in political terms. I said: "How would you like to go down in history, following a major catastrophe, as the official responsible for a lack of preparedness?" Those of you who deal with government officials hear responses similar to the ones I heard: "Earthquakes will not happen during my term in government, and I have more immediate budgetary needs to take care of." Or: "A cost/benefit analysis shows that only 500 people have died in this century from earthquakes in the United States. How can you justify such a large investment?" These are short-sighted views, and I think all of you know the answers to such questions.

I believe that concern about the public welfare is a primary role of a modern government, and in this sense natural hazard mitigation deserves attention with high priority. It is interesting to recall that in ancient China, dynasties fell after a major earthquake--as if the Emperor should have protected his people against such a catastrophe. I suppose the modern analog to that is the political process and the reaction of a citizenry that sees inadequate attention to hazard reduction. I believe that a modern government should not wait for a Tokyo of 1923 or a Tangshan of 1976 before it commits adequate resources. Certainly governments should support adequate research and development programs. They are needed and can return enormous benefits. R&D is really not terribly expensive in the scheme of things. The same can be said for public education and the preparation of construction codes. It is more difficult to deal with the larger financial resources, both public and private, that are needed with the implementation of construction codes or the replacement of unsafe buildings with new buildings that meet modern codes. This should be part of decision-making through the political process. I believe an educated citizenry will insist on an

19

adequate response from their governments. History will judge governments not only by their attention to health, education, and economic growth but also by preparing their countries in advance of natural disasters.

I would like to make a proposal to you on the occasion of this Eighth World Conference. It is a proposal to establish an International Decade of Hazard Reduction (IDHR). By way of background, let me remind you that natural hazards know no national boundaries except the earth itself, and that there is already a history of cooperation in earthquake engineering between nations, some examples of which are being reported on at this very conference. Cooperation between scientists and engineers is international by long tradition. The large number of scientists from so many different countries present today gives evidence to that. To counter some dangerous trends in competition between nations, worldwide cooperation on behalf of people everywhere would be an important symbol.

An IDHR would exploit many of the scientific and engineering advances of recent years. Research on natural hazards, particularly earthquake hazards, is moving to a new era characterized by theoretical advances, large-scale field experiments, expensive experimental testing facilities, use of supercomputers, access to global monitoring and communication facilities. At the same time hazards research in many countries is funded below the level that is really needed to fully utilize these new opportunities.

In view of these observations, I believe there is great need, and much support can be found, to establish an International Decade of Hazard Reduction. This special initiative would see all nations joining forces to reduce the consequences of natural hazards. The planning could start within a year or two, with the preparation of national plans. The implementation could take place in a few years. Perhaps it would be appropriate for the final decade of this century. What better way to start the new millenium than a world better organized to reduce suffering.

What would be some of the features of IDHR? Earthquake hazards would be a major element of such a program. The earthquake professionals are well organized, witness this meeting. The field is positioned for making rapid advances, given the impetus of a dedicated, coordinated, international effort. For example, an international supercomputer facility dedicated to natural hazard research might be established. Machines with billions of floating point operations per second would be available by that time. With this level of computing power, one can think of expert systems for the design of structures using realistic non-linear models. One can think of calculations of ground motion based on realistic earthquake fault models and wave propagation models. One can envisage international teams undertaking the regionalization of risk. Many parts of the world that are particularly prone to earthquakes have not had the advantages of a risk assessment for their region.

National goals for participation in the international decade could be a major spur to country action. Think of what the International Geophysical Year some 25 years ago did for the field of geophysics in this country and your countries. As a significant bonus, an international program can improve the infrastructure for hazard mitigation in the developing countries where the problems are so severe, the dangers are so great, and the ability to respond is so poor. Experimental facilities that require high capital outlays and that contribute so much to our understanding of how to design and build buildings can be done on an international basis, perhaps using the CERN models developed for particle physics. Costs would be shared and access would be provided to all countries. Another component might be a global strong motion network with standardized instruments. Another feature might be a plan for international cooperation in providing post-disaster relief.

The world is more vulnerable to cataclysms today than ever before because of the growing population, the concentration of population, the fragility of lifelines, and the interdependence of people. Our knowledge of the effects of great cataclysms is growing. For example, there is growing concern about a new source of danger--resurgent calderas. These are huge volcanic collapse features which combine the destructiveness of earthquakes as well as huge volcanic eruptions. Imagine events that are 1000 times more powerful than the eruption of Mt. St. Helens, which itself caused damage of over a billion and a half dollars. Some resurgent calderas are showing renewed activity in the form of surface doming, earthquake swarms and evidence of magma accumulating a few kilometers beneath the surface. The geologic record tells us that the occurrence rate might be about ten per million years. The destructiveness of some resurgent calderas can be measured in millions of square miles of agricultural land wiped out by the ash deposits, the lofting of fine ash and the sulfur products into high atmosphere, blotting out the sun for perhaps weeks at a time, producing worldwide agricultural losses. An IDHR would include studies of resurgent calderas, earthquakes, cometary impacts, storms, and other destructive natural phenomena.

Some concluding thoughts. By any measure, civilization has made much progress in this millenium. I think the world is better off today than it was 100 years ago, certainly better off than it was 500 years ago. If you have any doubts, as some do, think in terms of life expectancies and how they have improved, of the elimination of famines, the elimination of epidemics, and the remarkable economic progress. Science and technology has been the major factor responsible for the improved state of humankind. Yet much remains to be done. We are haunted by the specter of natural hazards, with immense consequences, because of concentrated populations, frailty of modern social institutions, and the other factors that I have mentioned. Some major earthquakes are expected in the next few years. Indeed, they may be "overdue"! Can we minimize their destructiveness? Most of you will agree with me that we will have the technical means to do so in the years ahead.

Indeed, humankind has the technical means to achieve great things in this next millenium: We can provide an adequate food supply, conquer disease once and for all, provide global education, extend economic progress, and greatly reduce the risk of natural hazards. Most important--we can eliminate war so that the worst hazard of all--nuclear war--is no longer a threat. I believe we can and must progress in this manner. Perhaps this is our last opportunity to do so. I believe that the involvement of dedicated scientists and engineers, such as those gathered in this room today, is the key to achieving these essential global goals.

Thank you very much.

Penzien - The next presentation in these opening ceremonies is the Conference Lecture to be given by George Housner.[*]

In selecting him, we are recognizing a person who, over his 50 year professional career, has stood as a giant among those advancing earthquake engineering from its infancy ito a well established discipline in engineering and applied science.

There is hardly a topic of importance in earthquake engineering to which Professor Housner has not given serious thought. Many of us know this well, for we have been privileged to follow his research contributions since early days, as they were appearing in the literature and at conferences.

He has been an inspiration to generations of students and researchers not only at the California Institute of Technology, his home institution, but throughout the world.

Through his participation as a consultant on a number of important engineering projects in several countries, Professor Housner has contributed to the improvement of seismic design practice. During this week many of you will have an opportunity to use the San Francisco Bay Area Rapid Transit System, a project which had the benefit of his advice when its planning started 25 years ago.

Apart from his many important technical contributions to the advancement of earthquake engineering, Professor Housner's foresight and vision have given direction to the U.S. national program of earthquake hazards mitigation. The research community in the United States is especially grateful to him for his dedication and leadership in promoting support for earthquake engineering research.

---

[*] This introduction of Professor G.W. Housner is based, in part, on the 'citation' prepared by M.S. Agbabian and A.S. Veletsos, when he received the Medal of the Seismological Society of America in 1981.

Professor Housner has served as President of the Earthquake Engineering Research Institute, the host organizataion for this Conference, from 1954 to 1965; of the International Association for Earthquake Engineering from 1969 to 1973; and of the Seismological Society of America in 1977.

As would be expected, Professor Housner has received numerous awards and honors for his contibutions. I will not take time to go over the long list, but it is worthy of note that he was elected a member of the U.S. National Academy of Engineering in 1965, only one year after the Academy was founded; and to the U.S. National Academy of Sciences in 1972.

In this brief review this morning, it has clearly not been possible for me to highlight all of Professor Housner's contributions and to convey to you the significance of his impact and imprint on the advancement of earthquake engineering, especially in the United States. If I were to take the time to discuss all of his contributions it could become my narration of the history of earthquake engineering, in which he has played a most distinguished role. Instead, I will request George Housner to speak to us now on "The History of Earthquake Engineering".

CONFERENCE LECTURE

HISTORICAL VIEW OF EARTHQUAKE ENGINEERING
BY
G. W. HOUSNER, CALIFORNIA INSTITUTE OF TECHNOLOGY

Earthquake engineering is a 20th Century development, so recent that it is yet premature to attempt to write its history. Many persons in many countries have been involved in the development of earthquake engineering and it is difficult, if not impossible to identify the contributions of each. Many advances in the subject are not well-documented in the literature, and some of the documentation is misleading, or even incorrect. For example, in some instances, earthquake requirements were adopted in building codes but were not used by architects and engineers. And in other instances earthquake design was done by some engineers before seismic requirements were put in the code. A history of earthquake engineering written now could not present a satisfactory account because of poorly documented facts and, in addition, there are still many people that remember relevant information and would be severe critics of a history. To write an acceptable history, it is necessary to wait till most of the poorly known facts have disappeared from memory and literature, then, with a coherent blend of fact and fiction, history can be written.

Although 1984 is too soon to write a definitive history, it is an appropriate time for an historical view of earthquake engineering development to see where we were, where we now are, and where we are going. In this regard, it is interesting to compare the Eighth World Conference with the First World Conference on Earthquake Engineering. In 1956, the 50th anniversary of the San Francisco earthquake, the First World Conference was held in the city of Berkeley, California. It is indicative of the very recent development of earthquake engineering that many of those pioneers who attended the First Conference are also present, 28 years later, at the Eighth Conference. It is gratifying to see that the

attendance at 8WCEE is more than 10 times as large as the number attending 1WCEE. In the Preface to the Proceedings of the First Conference, the President of EERI said "The world conference on earthquake engineering was originated and planned by EERI for the purpose of 1) Observing by an appropriate technical meeting the 50th anniversary year of the destructive San Francisco earthquake of 1906 and, 2) Bringing together the scientists and engineers from major seismic areas of the world in order that their knowledge of earthquakes and developments in the science and art of earthquake-resistant design and construction might be pooled for the benefit of all mankind." And this still represents the purpose of the Eighth Conference. However, a big change has occurred in the number of papers presented. The Proceedings of the First Conference had 40 papers and the Proceedings of the Eighth Conference contain 844 papers. This 20 times increase in the number of persons seriously studying earthquake engineering is indicative of the increased importance of the subject in the seismic countries of the world. The authors in the First Conference came from 11 countries and the authors in the Eighth Conference came from 42 countries. Very few seismic countries are not represented at the 1984 Conference and this indicates that there are few seismic countries that are not actively trying to protect against destructive earthquakes, and this is a great change from the situation in 1956.

EARLY DAYS OF EARTHQUAKE ENGINEERING

In viewing the early days of earthquake engineering, it is not appropriate to consider developments in pure seismology but, rather, restrict consideration to developments which were made by engineers or which have a special relevance to earthquake engineering. It is surprising to learn that in the early days the most prominent men in earthquake engineering were almost all natives of England, a country of low seismicity. This can be attributed to the Industrial Revolution, in which England was a pioneering country. The intellectual excitement associated with rapid developments in all of engineering between the years 1700-1900 attracted the attention of many able men and some

27

developed an interest in earthquakes. Robert Hooke (1635-1703), the discoveror of Hooke's Law, which is well-known in engineering, gave a series of lectures at the Royal Society in 1667-68 which were published in book form in 1705 with the title "Lectures and Discourses of Earthquakes and Subterranean Eruptions". This was before the days of earthquake engineering and Hooke was actually considering geological matters when he argued that the raising of sub-acqueous land into mountains was caused by earthquakes, so it might be said that Hooke took the first step along the path that led to the theory of plate tectonics. Also, Thomas Young (1773-1829), of Young's Modulus, in his book "Lectures on National Philosophy", vol. 2, 1807, gave what appears to be the first European bibliography of earthquake publications. It is interesting that both Hooke and Young, who are so well known by engineers, should have studied earthquakes, though in those early days it was premature to think about earthquake engineering.

In the 19th Century, a number of English engineers developed a keen interest in earthquakes, including Robert Mallet (1810-81), a civil engineer, John Milne (1850-1913), a mining engineer, James Ewing (1855-?) and Thomas Gray (1850-1908), both mechanical engineers. In the last century no distinction was made between seismology and earthquake engineering. In fact, the word "seismology" derived from the Greek work "seismos-shaking", was invented by the engineer Robert Mallet and covered all the various interests in earthquakes: earthquake occurrence, ground shaking, earthquake damage, etc. It seems that the name "seismology" (= shake-knowledge) originally designated what we would call earthquake engineering, and it was only during later developments that the name came to designate the studies of the non-engineering aspects of the subject. Robert Mallet also coined the terms "epicenter", "seismic focus", "isoseismal line", and "meizoseismal area".

Robert Mallet published his first paper, "On the Dynamics of Earthquakes" in the Transactions of the Irish Academy, vol. 2, 1848. In this paper he discusses earthquake effects and considers seismic waves and tsunamis, and he also describes his invention of the electro-magnetic seismograph (see Figure 1). This instrument sat at rest till it sensed the arrival of the seismic waves which activated it and the response of the instrument was recorded on a rotating drum. Mallett did not build such an instrument but a modified seismograph along these lines was built in 1855 by Luigi Palmieri (1867-96) in Naples, Italy which actually made some earthquake records. Mallett also invented the "rocking blocks" (or falling pins) intensity meter, a form of which for many years was used by the construction industry to measure the intensity of ground motion generated by blasting; and he also compiled a seismic map of the world which was in use for many years. Mallet also studied the destructive Naples earthquake of 16 December 1857 and wrote a detailed report which included carefully drawn isoseismal lines. He also compiled a 600-page catalog of earthquakes which he said was the "first attempt to complete a catalog that shall embrace all recorded earthquakes". Robert Mallet, I believe, can be called the Primeval Earthquake Engineer.

Milne, Ewing and Gray[*] developed an interest in earthquakes while teaching at Imperial College of Engineering in Tokyo (later merged into Tokyo University). In addition to studying earthquake damage and other phenomena, they were pioneers in the design and construction of sensitive seismographs and the study of the seismograms. The work of these men, together with Japanese seismologists such as Seikei Sekiya (1855-96), the world's first officially appointed professor of seismology, and Fusakichi Omori (1868-?) led to modern seismology. The Seismological Society of Japan was organized by these men in 1880 and this first earthquake society was the forerunner of the many National Societies of Earthquake Engineering that make up the International Association for Earthquake Engineering.

In the latter part of the 19th century and the early part of the 20th century, some large and important earthquakes occurred that aroused the interests of engineers and seismologists and marked an important

---

[*] Thomas Gray later emigrated to the United States and from 1888 to 1908 was professor of engineering mechanics at Rose Polytechnic Institute in Indiana.

phase of earthquake engineering. These were the 1891 Mino-Awari, Japan; the 1906 San Francisco, California; and the 1908 Messina, Italy earthquakes. The Mino-Awari earthquake left a prominent fault scarp which is still shown in books on seismology and the San Francisco earthquake focused attention on the San Andreas fault and its displacement. Although these two large earthquakes received worldwide attention, the time was not yet ready for earthquake engineering. In his 1907 ASCE paper "The Effects of the San Francisco Earthquake of April 18, 1906 on Engineering Construction", Professor Charles Derleth said" "An attempt to calculate earthquake stress is futile. Such calculations could lead to no practical conclusions of value". Engineering thinking was still based in a static world and dynamics seemed yet to be unthinkable. Despite the fact that in 1906 California had a small population with no great cities, the damage caused by the earthquake was $10-$20 billion (1980) dollars though the number of deaths was only about 1,000. This did not shock engineers into developing earthquake engineering. In 1908, however, a large earthquake devastated the city of Messina, Italy and surrounding area, with a loss of life of 83,000, and this disaster was responsible for the birth of practical earthquake design of structures.

It appears that prior to December 28, 1908 engineering thinking was not ready for grappling with the engineering design of structures to resist earthquakes. In most seismic regions, the common type of construction was masonry buildings, low in height. At that date, the use of reinforced concrete, and the use of structural steel, was still in its infancy, and the education of engineers was not of a type to encourage thinking about earthquake forces and stresses.

MESSINA, ITALY EARTHQUAKE OF DECEMBER 28, 1908

As the population of the world increases, the number of structures at risk also increases, and the number of people exposed to earthquake hazards increases. This leads to the possibility of great disasters. The 83,000 death toll of the Messina earthquake was the greatest number ever from a European earthquake. Even the famous 1775 Lisbon, Portugal earthquake had fewer deaths (60,000). The government of Italy responded to the Messina earthquake by appointing a special committee composed of nine practicing engineers and five professors of engineering to study the earthquake and to make recommendations. The report of this committee appears to be the first engineering recommendation that earthquake-resistant structures be designed by means of the equivalent static method (%g method). This portion of the report appears to have been the contribution of M. Panetti, Professor of Applied Mechanics in Turin, and he recommended that the first story be designed for a horizontal force equal to 1/12 the weight above and the second and third stories to be designed for 1/8 of the building weight above. He stated that the problem is really one of dynamics which, however, is so complicated that it is necessary to have recourse to a static method. Also, in 1909, A. Danusso, Professor of Structural Engineering at Milan, won a prize with his paper, "Statics of Anti-Seismic Construction". The method recommended by Panetti and explained by Danusso, gradually spread to seismic countries around the world. First it was used by progressive engineers and later was adopted by building codes. Until the 1940's it was the standard method of design required by building codes. In Japan, the method was applied successfully to reinforced concrete buildings by Professor Tachu Naito prior to the 1923 Tokyo earthquake and, in the late 1920's, it was applied by Professor R.R. Martel in the design of a 12-story steel-frame building in Los Angeles. Following the Tokyo earthquake the static method of design with seismic coefficient of 10% was adopted by the Japanese building ordinance and, following the 1933 Long Beach earthquake, the city of Los Angeles adopted the method with a coefficient of 8%. On January 1, 1943, the City of Los Angeles changed its earthquake requirements so that the seismic coefficient varied over the height of the building and was also a function of the total height (i.e. the period of vibration). This was the first time that the seismic requirements of a building code took into account the flexibility of a building as well as its mass; and these requirements were based on dynamic analyses of structures, carried out by R.R. Martel and his students, under research grants made by the Los Angeles County Department of Building and Safety.

31

The 1923 Tokyo earthquake was also responsible for the establishment of the Earthquake Research Institute at Tokyo University with an eminent engineer, Professor Kyoji Suyehiro, as the first director. This was the first research group formed to study earthquake engineering and seismology.

RECORDING AND ANALYZING STRONG EARTHQUAKE SHAKING

The recording of earthquake ground accelerations was often recommended by engineers who studied the problem of designing for earthquakes, including John Milne, Kyoji Suyehiro, R.R. Martel and others. However, it seems that prior to 1925 the technology of seismic instruments was not adequate to building strong-motion accelerographs and even in the later 1920's the mental and financial inertia was too great for an accelerograph to be developed. We owe the first accelerographs to the eminent engineer John R. Freeman (1855-1932) who became interested in earthquakes in 1925 at the age of 70, and who attended the 1929 World Engineering Conference in Tokyo where he met and became friends with Martel and Suyehiro. He immediately understood the need for a strong-motion accelerograph and strongly recommended to the Secretary of Commerce that such an instrument should be designed and constructed. On March 11, 1930, Secretary Lamont, an engineer, stated in a letter to Freeman that it would be done. The first accelerographs were installed by the Seismological Field Survey of the U.S. Coast and Geodetic Survey in late 1932, just in time to record the strong ground shaking of the destrutive March 10, 1933 Long Beach earthquake. This was a most important step in the development of earthquake engineering. For the first time engineers could see the nature of strong ground shaking: the amplitude of motion, the frequency characteristics, and the duration of shaking. These were items of great interest and they cleared up much confusion, as the literature prior to 1933 contained many erroneous estimates of these quantities. We, who live in 1984, can hardly conceive of the difficulty of estimating these quantities 100 years ago when the world had not yet moved into the modern age. For example, in the Transactions of the Seismological Society of Japan a paper by J. MacGowan on

"Earthquakes in China" describes the earthquake of June 12, 1878 which occurred near Suchow, and he said that it was reported that in Suchow the "shaking was felt for the space of time taken in swallowing 1/2 bowl of rice". At the time of the First World Conference in 1956, fewer than 70 strong-motion accelerographs were installed in the world, and at that time, few destructive earthquakes occurred close to an accelerograph. It is significant that now most seismic countries have installed networks of accelerographs and that important records are being obtained in many countries. We now have a much better understanding of earthquake ground motions and their effects. In addition, many accelerographs are now installed on structures to record their motions during earthquakes, and these have demonstrated the dynamic responses of multistory buildings, bridges, dams, etc.

The development of computers, first the analog type and then the digital type, was very important for earthquake engineerng. These made possible the practical analysis of accelerograms, for without computers the analysis was exceedingly slow and laborious. Computers made possible the development of the response spectrum of earthquake motions and the design spectrum which have played important roles in earthquake engineering and have been adopted in other branches of engineering also. Computers have also made possible the calculation of the dynamic response of structures to earthquake ground shaking and this has greatly clarified our understanding of structural dynamics. We are now able to make dynamic analyses of complex structures. The finite element method of analysis has also been an important development for earthquake engineering. The widespread installation of strong-motion accelerographs, together with the development of powerful computers, has provided large amounts of data and this poses problems of data acquisition, data analysis, data storage, data retrieval, and also data understanding.

In retrospect, it can be seen that in the last twenty years earthquake engineering has been strongly influenced by the implementation of major projects, such as: nuclear power plants, highrise buildings, major dams, offshore oil drilling platforms, longspan bridges, LNG storage tanks, etc. The large cost of these projects and the need for a high degree of safety required a level of earthquake analysis and design much higher than for ordinary structures. As a consequence, the development of earthquake engineering was accelerated by the needs of these special projects.

DEVELOPMENT OF BUILDING CODES

Special structures such as high-rise buildings, major dams, LNG storage tanks, etc., because of their critical importance are usually analyzed and designed by making use of the latest research developments. On the other hand, ordinary structures which compose the bulk of modern construction are usually designed according to the requirements of a building code. Because the code is a legal document that specifies a minimum level of design that must be attained by structures, and because it has a large socio-economic impact, substantial changes in code requirements are made slowly and cautiously. In addition, because the building code affects so many agencies, groups, individuals, etc. there is a great inertia against change and developments in the building code tend to lag behind developments in research. In many instances, needed changes in the code are deferred until the occurrence of a destructive earthquake; for example, 1908 Messina, Italy; 1923 Tokyo, Japan; 1933 Long Beach, California; 1971 San Fernando, California; 1976 Tangshan, China. The development of the building code thus illustrates the development of applied earthquake engineering for ordinary construction. The development of earthquake requirements in the Los Angeles city building code is a good example. Until 1933, earthquake design was not required; then the deaths and damage caused by the M6.3 March 10, 1933 Long Beach earthquake produced the requirement that every building must be designed for a minimum horizontal force of 8% of the weight, without consideration of height, shape, rigidity, material of construction, use, foundation condition, or degree of seismic hazard. The code was changed at intervals and the requirements of the present code do take into account the foregoing items. In addition, following the 1971 San Fernando earthquake a requirement was added that every structure over 160 feet in height shall have strength sufficient to resist the effects of earthquakes as determined by a dynamic analysis, and that this analysis shall be based on the ground shaking prescribed by a soil-geology-seismology report. The 1984 Los Angeles code is a great improvement over the 1934 code. The past fifty years, which is a short time in the life of a building code, have seen great improvements in building codes worldwide; and these improvements will certainly reduce loss of life and property damage in future earthquakes. During the past 100 years, over one million persons have been killed by earthquakes and it is the responsibility of earthquake engineers to ensure that this does not happen again during the coming 100 years. Earthquake engineers should examine the building codes in their countries to make sure that the requirements are indeed appropriate to the seismic risk.

NON-TECHNICAL EARTHQUAKE ENGINEERING

A history of earthquake engineering should also examine the development of thinking in governmental agencies, and the thinking of the public. Relatively recent developments in some cities, such as Tokyo and Los Angeles, include improved thinking in city government agencies. National and state government agencies are also giving earthquake hazards increasing consideration. In some regions, earthquake preparedness measures are being taken to reduce the risk of life and property, to prepare to handle the emergency when the coming earthquake occurs, and to mitigate the effects of future earthquake disasters upon the functioning of the city and the impact on the public. These are noteworthy developments in non-technical earthquake engineering, if we define earthquake engineering broadly to encompass all non-technical, as well as technical, efforts directed toward minimizing those harmful effects of earthquakes.

Public understanding of earthquake risk is also important. A great advance in earthquake knowledge possessed by the average citizen has occurred over the past thirty years, and this has resulted in greater support for earthquake preparedness measures. However, even today, the average citizen has a relatively poor understanding of earthquake risks and earthquake engineering benefits. Because of the way the news media handle the topic of earthquakes, the public tends to oscillate between excessive alarm and excessive complacency. Improvements need to be made in public education about earthquake risks and earthquake preparedness, beginning with children in the public schools.

SUMMARY

Over the past fifty years, there has been remarkable progress in earthquake engineering research. Knowledge of earthquake ground shaking and earthquake vibrations of structures has undergone a great expansion. Advances in methods of dynamic analysis enable the earthquake response of planned structures to be calculated. Experimental research is providing valuable data on the physical properties of structures and structural elements. The increase in number of research papers published each year is indicative of the progress being made. We have now attained a good understanding of the elastic earthquake response of typical buildings. However, there are many special structures, industrial equipment, etc. whose earthquake survival is important and which need special earthquake engineering research. Also, the question of "maximum credible" or "maximum probable" earthquake needs to be better defined by research, as well as the question of appropriate level of design of structures for such events of low likelihood. And more research needs to be done on designing for controlled damage in the event of large, infrequent earthquakes.

Building codes have also undergone a big development over the past fifty years. The 1984 building codes now handle the earthquake design of structures in a much improved way over the 1934 building codes. However, the real test of a building code comes when a city experiences strong ground shaking. Actual structures, as distinguished from ideal structures, are so complex that their behavior must be tested by strong shaking to establish their adequacy or to reveal inadequacies. In 1984, conclusive tests of modern building codes have not yet been made. It is important that, in the future, destructive earthquakes be studied with a view to assessing the adequacy of the building code. Many earthquakes have been inspected in the past, and many reports have been written, but too few valuable conclusions have been deduced. Earthquake engineers should prepare ahead of time to learn from coming destructive earthquakes. Thought must be given ahead of time to what can be learned, and preparations should be made ahead of time for the learning process.

When the earthquake comes, everything connected to the earth either directly, or indirectly, will be shaken. All those items whose survival is very important must be given special attention in design and construction to insure against unacceptable damage, and structures must also be designed to protect against injury and loss of life. An earthquake disaster requires three things: 1) the occurrence of an earthquake sufficiently large to produce strong ground shaking; 2) the earthquake must be sufficiently close so that a city experiences strong shaking; and 3) the city must be unprepared for an earthquake, with numerous weak buildings. When these three coincide there is a disaster. Such coincidences were not uncommon in the past, for example,

Earthquake Location	Date	Magnitude	Approx. No. of Deaths
Hokaido, Japan	Dec. 30, 1730	?	137,000
Calcutta, India	1737	?	300,000
Lisbon, Portugal	Nov. 1, 1755	8+	60,000
Syria	Oct. 30, 1759	?	30,000
Calabria, Italy	Feb. 5, 1783	?	30,000
Peru-Ecuador	Feb. 4, 1797	?	40,000
Kangr, India	Apr. 4, 1905	?	19,000
San Francisco	Apr. 18, 1906	8.3	1,000
Santiago, Chile	Aug. 17, 1906	8.6	20,000
Messina, Italy	Dec. 28, 1908	7.5	83,000
Avezzano, Italy	Jan. 13, 1915	7	30,000
Kansu, China	Dec. 16, 1920	8.6	100,000
Tokyo, Japan	Sep. 1, 1923	8.3	100,000
Bihar, India	Jan. 15, 1934	8.4	11,000
Taiwan	Apr. 20, 1935	7.1	3,000
Quetta, Pakistan	May 30, 1935	7.5	30,000
Chile	Jan. 25, 1939	8.3	28,000
Erzincan, Turkey	Dec. 26, 1939	7.9	30,000
Ambato, Ecuador	Aug. 5, 1949	6.8	6,000
Agadir, Morocco	Feb. 29, 1960	5.8	10,000
Quazin, Iran	Sep. 1, 1962	7.0	12,000
Tangshan, China	Jul. 28, 1976	7.8	250,000+

The foregoing list is incomplete; many other destructive earthquakes occurred where death tolls numbered in the thousands. Disastrous earthquakes can be expected also in future years, for many existing cities are poorly prepared to resist earthquakes. In addition, inasmuch as the world's population is increasing by 80 million persons per year and cities are correspondingly expanding, the earthquake risk is increasing. In coming years large earthquakes can be expected to occur close to large cities more frequently than in the past. It is the responsibility of earthquake engineers to insure that the new construction in these cities is earthquake resistant, and that the greatest hazards from old weak buildings are eliminated. The discipline of earthquake engineering is now entering its golden age with greatly expanded knowledge and capabilities, but it is also facing important new problems, for in coming years there will be construction of large, complex, and costly structures, industrial facilities, and socio-economic projects which the earthquake engineer must make safe against destructive ground shaking.

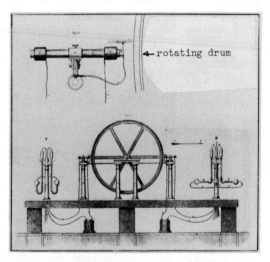

Figure 1. Drawing of Robert Mallet's proposed seismograph (1848). The seismic elements, two horizontal and one vertical, are tubes of mercury which are excited into oscillation by the earthquake. The oscillation of the mercury makes and breaks an electric circuit and this activates a spring-loaded solenoid to press a pencil against a rotating drum thus recording the time of making or breaking the circuit. This would give some information about the oscillations of the mercury.

References

The Founders of Seismology, Charles Davison, Cambridge University Press, 1927.

Earthquake Damage and Earthquake Insurance, John R. Freeman, McGraw-Hill, 1932.
Elementary Seismology, C.F. Richter, Freeman, 1958.

International Dictionary of Geophysics, K. Runcorn, Ed., Pergamon Press, 1967.

Seismic Codes and Procedures, G.V. Berg, EERI, 1982.

The Early History of Seismometry, J. Dewey & P. Byerly, Bulletin of Seismological Society, Feb. 1969.

Transactions of the Seismological Society of Japan, Vols. 1-16, 1880-96, Yokohama.

Penzien - I now request Professor Housner to return to the podium to present a special award on behalf of EERI, to Dr. Kiyoshi Muto.

PRESENTATION OF THE EERI AWARD TO DR. KIYOSHI MUTO

BY
GEORGE HOUSNER

It is a great pleasure to make this presentation of the EERI award to Dr. Kiyoshi Muto at the opening ceremony of the Eighth World Conference on Earthquake Engineering. His long, productive career entitles Dr. Muto to be called "The Senior Citizen of Earthquake Engineering." Engineers living in seismic countries have a responsibility to develop earthquake protection and Dr. Muto has accepted this responsibility and has done much to protect the citizens of Japan against earthquakes and, through diffusion of information, has also contributed to the safety of peoples throughout the world. As a young man, he studied the 1923 Tokyo earthquake, and I believe this event made him an earthquake engineer. In addition to studying the 1923 Tokyo earthquake damage, he performed a

notable analysis of the survey measurements of the floor of Tokyo Bay (Sagami Bay). These survey measurements indicated extremely large tectonic displacements resulting from the earthquake but, by means of his analysis, Dr. Muto was able to show that the true displacements were smaller and quite different. So over the past 61 years, from 1923 to 1984, Dr. Muto has demonstrated his ability and productivity as an earthquake engineer.

Dr. Muto served for many years as Professor of Structural Engineering at Tokyo University and also served a term as Dean of the Engineering School. He is widely known for having developed the Muto method of structural analysis of building frames for resisting lateral forces. He also served as Chairman of the Strong-Motion Accelerograph Committee which developed the SMAC accelerograph which is now so widely installed in Japan. He has received many honors during his career, including the giving of an invited lecture before the Emperor of Japan. After retiring as professor, he became the first Director of the newly-formed research laboratory of the Kajima Construction Company, and while there he was responsible for the development of the slit shear wall for earthquake resistance of high-rise buildings. Later he formed the Muto Institute of Mechanics which is an active research and consulting organization dealing with advanced problems in earthquake engineering. I recall that after the First World Conference in 1956, when I was President of EERI, Dr. Muto wrote to me saying that the time seemed right to form an international association for earthquake engineering, and it was agreed that he should proceed with the organization of the association. Dr. Muto and his co-workers drafted the first statutes of the International Association for Earthquake Engineering and he served as the first president. We may therefore say that Dr. Muto is the father of IAEE.

Dr. Muto has had an active career that spans over 60 years, and I think it is fair to say that during these years earthquakes were never far from his mind, and that a large percentage of the projects he undertook were related to earthquake engineering. In addition to his technical work, Dr. Muto served on many committees related to earthquake engineering and his contributions had a very positive influence on the development of earthquake engineering. Dr. Muto's career richly deserves the recognition of earthquake engineers throughout the world.

Dr. Muto, on behalf of the Earthquake Engineering Research Institute, I present to you this engraved bronze plaque which recognizes your many contributions to earthquake engineering.

RESPONSE BY DR. K. MUTO

Mr. Chairman, and Distinguished Guests:

I wish to say thank you ever so much to the members of this organizing committee and to you all concerned, for offering me this glorious moment.

Thank you!

CONCLUDING REMARKS
BY
DR. J. PENZIEN

Before bringing these opening ceremonies to a close, I should like to express sincere thanks and appreciation, on behalf of the Steering Committee, to the many organizations and groups of individuals that have contributed to the financing and planning of the Conference.

First, I should like to single out the U.S. National Science Foundation which deserves special recognition. Through its Earthquake Hazard Mitigation Program, it funds most of the earthquake engineering research conducted in the United States. Many of the papers being presented at this Conference are a direct result of NSF funded projects. In addition to this indirect support, NSF has provided the largest amount of funds of any single donor in direct support of the Conference. I hereby acknowledge this support and express our deep appreciation to the NSF representatives here today.

I wish time would permit me to single out each of the other donors to this Conference and to be specific about their activities in earthquake engineering. Unfortunately, time does not permit me to do so. I do however wish to acknowledge the major support provided by:

Bechtel Group, Inc.

John A. Blume

California Department of Water Resources

Chevron U.S.A. Inc.

Electric Power Research Institute

International Business Machines Corporation

U. S. Army Corps of Engineers

U. S. Federal Emergency Management Agency

U. S. Geological Survey

U.S. National Science Foundation

U. S. Nuclear Regulatory Commission

To their representatives here today, I express our heartfelt thanks and appreciation. Also to the many other organizations and individuals that made donations to our Conference, I likewise express our gratitude and thanks.

Turning my attention now to those groups and individuals who have worked so very hard, with total dedication to the Conference, it is impossible to give them adequate recognition and thanks at this time. More than 70 people serving on 8 organizing committees have been involved in the planning. You will find their names listed under the various committee titles at the back of your Final Program. To these individuals and to their affiliate organizations that have provided much support, let us join together in expressing our thanks and appreciation.

Finally, I wish to extend my own personal thanks to the members of the Steering Committee. I have never worked with a more competent, cooperative, and dedicated group of individuals. It has been a pleasure working with them.

These Opening Ceremonies are now closed. Thank you.

II. INVITED LUNCHEON ADDRESSES

a. Seismology as a Factor in Earthquake Engineering

Dr. Bruce Bolt—July 24, 1984

b. Influence of Seismic Environment on
Design of Major Structures

Dr. Jai Krishna—July 27, 1984

SEISMOLOGY AS A FACTOR IN EARTHQUAKE ENGINEERING[*]

Bruce A. Bolt(I)

INTRODUCTION

I appreciate this opportunity to present to this distinguished group of earthquake engineers from around the world a personal commentary on the contribution of seismology to their discipline. I would like to begin by recalling a comment by a professor of engineering made to me two decades ago. He said that modern engineering was in debt to earthquake and wind forces in making the subject a field of dynamics rather than statics, and thereby attracting some of the brightest minds to the discipline. Perhaps it is in this sense that engineering owes most to seismology!

Because it seems to be the tradition both in seismology and engineering to rely on various scales, such as the Modified Mercalli intensity scale and the Richter magnitude scale, at the outset I shall define a scale to measure the size of the factor in the title of this talk. Let us then define the Mallett scale, named after one of the founders of seismology who was also to be an engineer. The scale will run from one to ten and be a measure of the degree of integration between seismological and earthquake engineering activity. We may now proceed to analyze the growth of seismology from its early days in the middle of the last century to its present form, concentrating on the contributions it has made to the design of structures engineered to resist strong earthquake motion.

(I) Professor of Seismology, University of California, Berkeley, California 94720
* Luncheon Lecture delivered at the 8WCEE on July 24, 1984.

THE BEGINNINGS OF SEISMOLOGY AND EARTHQUAKE ENGINEERING

In the modern scientific sense, both subjects were born together through the work of the Irish engineer, Robert Mallett, who as early as 1846 read a paper before the Irish Academy on the dynamics of earthquakes. The great Neopolitan earthquake of December 16, 1857, in southern Italy, provided him with the opportunity to make extensive field studies of seismic effects and to apply critically his engineering training to broad earthquake problems.

During his three-month visit to the damaged area, Mallett established much of the basis of observational field seismology. This he presented in a major report entitled "The Great Neopolitan Earthquake of 1857: The First Principles of Observational Seismology." Its flavor is given by this quotation: "When the observer first enters upon one of those earthquake shaken towns, he finds himself in the midst of utter confusion. He wanders over masses of dislocated stone and mortar... houses seem to have been precipitated to the ground in every direction. There seems to be no governing law. It is only by first gaining some commanding point, whence a general view over the whole field of ruin can be had and then by patient examination, house by house and street by street, analyzing each detail, that we at length perceive once and for all that this apparent confusion is but superficial." The whole attitude here is one of transferring earthquake studies from a stage of bewilderment to a systematic stage based on mechanical principles. At the end of his work, Mallett had coined much of the basic vocabulary, including hypocenter, isoseismal, wave path, and even seismology itself. Obviously at this time, interaction between seismology and earthquake engineering would be rated as ten on the Mallett scale.

This scientific method established by Mallett was developed by others through to the end of last century. The most notable figure in the tradition was John Milne. Milne was trained in mining and geology, with considerable mathematics, mechanics, geometric drawing and surveying, as well as geology and mineralogy, and practical instruction in workshops. When he was appointed Professor of Mining and Geology at the

Imperial College of Engineering in Tokyo in 1882, he began the great diversification of seismology seen in its modern form. Not only did he design sensitive seismographs and concern himself with the observation of earthquake waves from distant sources around the world, he was, also, greatly interested in what is today called strong-motion seismology. He was much affected by his field studies of the October 28, 1891, Mino-Owari earthquake, one of the largest and most devastating recorded in the modern era. Not only did it produce major surface fault ruptures, but wide-spread damage on the Nagoya-Gifu plain, about 140 miles west-southwest of Tokyo. Milne was concerned with the interaction between the wave motion and damage; a few days after the disaster he drew up a circular containing fifty queries on intensity and damage of direct interest to engineers. One result of the calamity was the creation, by the Emperor, of the Imperial Earthquake Investigation Committee. It consisted of engineers and architects, as well as professors of seismology, geology, mathematics, and physics at the University of Tokyo. Not only was it charged with ascertaining ways to predict earthquakes, but also with determining what could be done to minimize such disasters by the choice of more suitable methods of construction, building materials, and building sites.

Milne had already noted the importance of construction on earthquake damage and had set up specific apparatus to test various conclusions on design. He did experiments with models, trying to determine whether walls of a building which had once been cracked still continued to give way during further seismic shaking. He investigated the overturning and fracturing of mortar by horizontally applied motion and assisted in the construction of a metal-frame trolley on which high columns of bricks were built and vibrated by a system of cranks. In this work he collaborated with the great Japanese seismologist, Professor Omori. He also tested the idea of base isolation now much discussed in earthquake engineering and actually designed a building standing on cast-iron balls held between metal plates which separated the building from the pier supports. His instrumentation showed that slow-moving earth movements were transmitted to the building while sudden shocks were not.

These examples are sufficient to indicate that Milne, often designated "the father of modern seismology", made great contributions to what came to be called earthquake engineering. In his work we again see a rating close to the maximum on the Mallett scale.

A word should be said here on the effect of the 1906 San Francisco earthquake on seismological activity. Some of the major problems faced today stem from the absence of instruments in central California in 1906 which could record with fidelity the strong ground motion in that 8-1/4 earthquake. If such strong motion records had been obtained, much of the controversy regarding extrapolations from smaller earthquakes to ground motions expected in the largest earthquakes would not occur. The "Report" of the State Investigation Commission did, however, indicate the importance of trying to obtain such motions and efforts were made, for a time, to construct seismographs capable of remaining on scale during strong motion. One such instrument was designed subsequently by Professor C.F. Marvin and is still in place at the University of California at Berkeley. While it recorded some earthquakes, nothing of practical importance seems to have emerged.

THE FIRST GROWTH OF SEISMOLOGY

During the first forty years of the twentieth century, seismology achieved many important scientific results and became a crucial quantitative part of geophysics. In these years effective, sensitive seismographs were built and deployed around the world to record three components of seismic ground motions down to amplitudes of a few micrometers. From these global networks it became possible to locate remote earthquakes and hence build up objective catalogs of the world seismicity. Techniques to measure earthquake size by objective (instrumental) criteria emerged and the Richter magnitude scale was adopted with its subsequent amendments and improvements. During the thirties, the fault plane method of using the polarities of distant P waves was developed in the hands of Professor P. Byerly and his colleagues. This instrumental method led to the determination of the focal mechanisms of earthquake sources from distant recordings.

The work of many observational seismologists, in conjunction with theoretical and mathematical developments on elastic wave theory, led to the detailed interpretation of the wave forms on seismograms; the nomenclature of P, S, and surface waves was established and related to the structure of propagation path. Particularly at the hands of Sir Harold Jeffreys and Professor Beno Gutenberg, the scientific side of seismology led to the unraveling of the main discontinuities in the Earth's interior. Along somewhat different lines, seismic waves were used in the oil industry for exploration with major expenditures to develop seismic methods.

Strangely, at first sight, during this great advance in seismological activity, not much progress was made on the prediction of strong ground motion - the crucial information for dynamical analyses of engineered structures. I once asked Professor Perry Byerly why he had not given more attention to this aspect of seismology by, for example, examining more closely the wave forms in what is now called the near-field of the seismic sources. His response was that, if he had waited for another 1906 earthquake, he would still be an assistant professor of seismology. Clearly, the reason was that the sensitive seismographs were producing a great pool of new information on the transmission of seismic waves through the whole earth, while few data were available on the wave motion near to the seismic source itself.

The situation began to change after the 1933 Long Beach earthquake, when the first strong-motion record of modern type was obtained, showing quantitatively the time-history of accelerations of the ground in detail near to the wave source. This success led to a realization in the engineering field of the great value of such records. In most places around the world, the subject became part of engineering expertise, and credit is due to those engineers who struggled to obtain funds to extend the strong-motion instrument networks.

Nevertheless, up into the 1960's, although more strong-motion records became available, particularly from California earthquakes, seismologists, with few notable exceptions, did not interest themselves in this part of the subject. It was noted that the accelerograms were in general more complicated than ordinary seismograms. This complexity led to the claim that modeling of such seismic waves would best proceed in terms of stochastic ensembles of ground motion rather than the deterministic use of elastic wave theory that had been applied so successfully to the interpretations of sensitive seismographic motions.

MODERN STRONG-MOTION SEISMOLOGY

By the early 1960's, it had become clear that structural design, in earthquake prone regions, of large engineered structures, such as highrise buildings, large dams, and bridges, was advancing rapidly; seismic safety codes dictated that quantitative dynamical analyses be performed. Engineers began to ask penetrating questions concerning the seismological aspects of the input motion available to them. About this time, a standard record around the world was the 1940 El Centro strong-motion record, which was broadly accepted as characteristic of strong-motion, with peak accelerations of about 0.3g in the frequency range from 10 Hz down to 1 Hz. By the end of the decade, the spread of strong-motion instruments of less expensive design began to supply a variety of recordings of strong ground motions at various distances from the earthquake source, of earthquakes of moderate magnitudes. Sample attenuation curves of peak accelerations of rather simple type began to emerge.

After the late 1950's, in seismological circles, much emphasis was given, particularly in the United States, to methods of discriminating between underground nuclear explosions and natural earthquakes. Moreover, a new generation of standardized sensitive seismographs globally distributed, attracted researchers back to problems of earth structure and distant earthquakes. As a result, there was still little interaction between mainstream seismology and engineering. The Mallett scale value, until 1970, would perhaps have been as low as three to four.

As circumstantial evidence, I recall giving a lecture in the mid-1960's to a large audience of seismologists in Japan concerning aspects of strong ground motion, including an explanation for ground motions recorded in the 1966 Parkfield earthquake. The accelerometers measured a surprisingly high value of 0.5g in one horizontal component near and normal to the fault. After the lecture, a Japanese colleague told me that, while the discussion was interesting, in Japan it was not usual for seismologists to concern themselves with strong-motion records. These were regarded as a matter for engineering studies. (I hasten to add that that situation has greatly changed now in Japan and many important integrated studies on strong ground motion are made by leading seismologists in that country.)

A significant change took place after the 1971 San Fernando earthquake in southern California when hundreds of strong-motion records were obtained in this magnitude 6.5 earthquake. The most striking had a value of 1.2g horizontal acceleration near the abutment of Pacoima Dam. This record led to leading questions concerning topographic amplification of seismic waves and the types of wave involved in high peak accelerations. About the same time, wide use of digital computers meant that both seismologists and engineers could tackle more extensive computations and theoretical modeling. On the engineering side, response spectral computations, suggested originally by Professor G. Housner, became rapid and widely used; in seismology more realistic dislocation models were computed for the rupturing earthquake source. From both sides, the need emerged for improved recording equipment which would give high-fidelity measurements of strong ground motion under various conditions in the free field and in structures.

It should also be mentioned that, during this time, the need grew for dynamic analysis based on actual seismological inputs as a requirement of regulations involved in licensing critical structures. In particular in the United States, but also in other countries, nuclear regulatory agencies set strict criteria for seismological input, and seismic analysis demands led to the expenditures of large sums of money on strong-motion seismology and earthquake engineering.

Partly as a consequence of this work, it became clear that interpretations of many strong-motion records were feasible in terms of elastic wave and dislocation source theory. Even so, explanations for actual motions were not always unique and certain important aspects needed statistical rather than deterministic treatment.

During this drive for upgrading strong ground motion studies and research, new concepts were developed and firm criteria set. Inevitably the subject went down wrong roads as, for example, the decision to use peak acceleration of the ground as the dominant scaling factor for response spectra. This procedure focused attention on erratic parameters rather than on more stable measures of the kinematics of the ground motion suitable for engineering purposes.

We thus arrive at the present, with the introduction of digital seismographs providing a wide dynamic range and simple access to high-speed computers. Such instruments, with pre-event memories and radio receivers, allow direct time-correlated digital recording on cassettes, followed by rapid transition to standard magnetic tapes and standard format. Many of the reliable analog accelerometers are now operated in seismic areas around the world so that a steady stream of valuable records is coming to hand, from Japan, Italy, China, the U.S.A, and Mexico, to mention a few areas. In addition, special arrays of strong-motion seismographs have been designed in highly seismic areas of the world. Since 1978, a number of both variable and fixed-redundancy strong motion arrays have been installed. These arrays have immediate advantages. The P waves are not missed and complete seismograms of strong ground motion can be correlated spatially and temporally across the whole array. Research based on this extensive database is now pursued actively by both engineers and seismologists so that, at the present, a rating of seven or eight on the Mallett scale is reasonable.

FUTURE TRENDS

The occurrence of large earthquakes in large seismic areas of the world already instrumented will provide a rich source of data for analysis in the coming years. Seismologists in many countries are engaged with a vengeance in research on this data. Sophisticated modeling of seismic sources is being done by theoreticians in an attempt to reconstruct the recorded ground motion in various earthquakes. The hope is that engineers can be convinced that ground motion can be predicted for a given site at a given distance from a known earthquake source. Acceptance requires confidence, and such confidence is clearly not yet at a high level. There will need to be more discussion and interaction between earthquake engineers and seismologists, and both professions must learn the extent to which they can rely on the expertness of the other.

In this latter respect, it would be seen that broader educational opportunities should be set up within engineering schools to allow special integrated offerings on strong motion seismology. Such courses must give due regard to the requirements of engineers and to the limitations of the inferential aspects of seismic source modeling. There are many inherent uncertainties on the observational and theoretical sides, often due to the lack of knowledge of the precise geology and fault properties. At the same time, it may be that engineers need to rethink the kinds of parameters which they require for the input of their design calculations for multi-variant elastic and inelastic systems.

We look forward also to the extension of field measurements and numerical modeling of three-dimensional wave fields. Strong-motion instruments down boreholes are needed, particularly for problems to do with the variation of motion over small distances and the effects of soil on surface wave motions. Three-dimensional strong-motion arrays will also enable checks to be made on the seismological interpretation of accelerograms.

In all these matters, seismology and engineering are coming together. For example, in current problems of soil-structure interaction, the engineering models of a damped elastic structure attached to a flat horizontal layered elastic medium are not so different mathematically from the seismology model of an elastic ridge or mountain situated on a layered visco-elastic halfspace. We look forward in the next decade to reaching a Mallett scale rating near to ten - at least asymptotically.

REFERENCES

Anon., Earthquake Engineering Research. National Academy Press, Washington, D.C., 1982.

Bolt, B.A., The Interpretation of Strong Ground Motion Records, Office of Chief of Engineers, U.S. Army, Miscellaneous Report 17, U.S. Army Engineer Waterways Experiment Station S-73-1, 1981.

Herbert-Gustar, L.K., and P.A. Nott. John Milne, Father of Modern Seismology. Norbury, Tenterden, 1980.

Mallett, R. The Great Neopolitan Earthquake of 1857: The First Principles of Observational Seismology. Two volumes, Chapman & Hall, London, 1862.

INFLUENCE OF SEISMIC ENVIRONMENT ON DESIGNS OF MAJOR STRUCTURES[*]

JAI KRISHNA (I)

INTRODUCTION

This topic has two main facets - social impact of seismic environment on inhabitants of the area where a major structure is planned, and
the problems faced by the designers of the structure in making engineering decisions to ensure safety consistent with economy.

My personal background has been connected mainly with the major
structures involved in river-valley projects and therefore, I propose to
concentrate my remarks on some aspects of such structures, but most of
the influence is common to other structures as well.

What I say in this connection may not be of universal application
because the definition of a structure being 'major' may differ from
country to country. Similarly, how the influence of seismic environment
is going to affect the cost of structure will also vary with structure
and situation. At the same time the impact of a disaster caused by
neglecting these influences will also vary from place to place. But the
general concerns in choosing design parameters and the hurdles to be
crossed in doing so are quite similar everywhere. I would, therefore,
try to highlight these.

SOCIAL PROBLEM

An influence which is of common concern is the psychological impact
on the population of the area where a major structure is to be built in
a seismic environment. The fear of failure of the structure on account
of a severe earthquake will need to be dispelled by the designers,
particularly in India, where major river-valley projects lie in a very

---

(I) Professor Emeritus, University of Roorkee, Roorkee, U.P., India.
*   Luncheon Lecture delivered at the 8WCEE on July 27, 1984.

severe seismic zone along the Himalayas. In these areas bulk of the population has experienced earthquakes from time to time and have seen their dwellings crumble in some of them with considerable loss of life and property. The idea of the construction of a major structure like a dam with water stored at its back is a matter of great concern to the people there, as it would be everywhere in similar situations. The possibility of failure of such a structure is bound to disturb the social equilibrium and, in a democracy, could lead to protest and agitation. To alleviate fears, therefore, the extensive geological and seismological investigations undertaken to collect necessary data should be publicised widely to convince the public that every effort was being made to estimate the consequences of an earthquake on the structures and that adequate steps to ensure their safety would be taken by the designers.

Scientifically speaking, whereas geological and seismological studies give a lot of information, it is so far not feasible to pinpoint the possible location of a future earthquake around the site of any structure. There are very few distinctly visible faults like the San Andreas fault which are so active that even the history, covering a century gives sufficient information about its movement for engineering purposes. Let me refer to an area like the north-east of India which, in continuity with Burma in the south, China in the east and north, gets a large number of earthquakes. The Indian part alone had about 300 earthquakes of magnitude greater than 5 and going up to 8.6 in the last 150 years. The limited studies carried out on the faults there, however, do not indicate the same kind of measurable movements as it seems to be the case with San Andreas fault. Therefore, the area does not permit the same quality of prediction as it may be possible some day on a fault with distinctly known movements. The common man is interested in knowing from the scientists about the occurrence of earthquakes in the same way as they get information about weather or floods. This is, however, a distant goal for any faults yet. For the present, we must convince the people that we can estimate the type of ground motion that is expected from the earthquakes in a particular area and that we have the competence to design structures against such motions with adequate safety built in them. This is the first most important influence of seismic environment on the duties of a designer of a major project that is, the need for winning the confidence of the people of the area for his competence to safeguard their interests.

DESIGNER'S ENGINEERING PROBLEMS

A designer wants to estimate the ground motion at a site on account of probable future earthquakes originating from different fault features - near and distant - so that structures could be designed accordingly. The problems he faces in estimating it and the decisions he has to take, quite often arbitrarily, have great bearing on the design of major structures.

In a severe seismic zone like North-East India the swarm of past epicenters makes it quite clear that the designer must assume that one or more of the strongest earthquakes could occur in the life time of the structure from any of the fault features with its hypocenter nearest the site of the structure. This would naturally appear to be a very severe condition, the probability of which must be low, but all the same, this has to be assumed to be the upper limit of the severity of design provisions, because the frequency of occurrence of earthquakes in this region is high (more than 300 shocks of magnitude higher than 5 in 150 years).

There are large areas of south India (about 15 times the size of North-East India) where the historical and geological evidence indicates the occurrence of a very few shocks spread over the whole region during the last 150 years (about 40 shocks greater than magnitude 5 but never greater than 6.5). Compared with North-East India the incidence of shocks here is 13% by numbers, less than 1% per unit area and less than 1/20th of a percent by the amount of energy release per unit area. Even in such areas a major structure - a dam or an atomic power plant, a refinery or a steel plant - is important enough to be designed for a strong earthquake. We were warned against ignoring such a possibility by Koyna earthquake of 1967, in which a very well-built concrete dam was damaged to an extent that heavy loss of agricultural and industrial production took place. In this area, of course, we could take magnitude 6.5 as the maximum credible shock, but in North-East India, it will be a commonly occurring size (40 shocks of size 6.5 to 8.5 in 150 years).

Here, we may take note of the fact that the maximum intensity of ground motion in the epicentral region may increase only marginally for shocks of magnitudes greater than 6.5 to about 7.25, and, but not appreciably beyond it, but the area covered by high intensity motion increases enormously. Thus for a major structure in South India, a respectable distance of about 20 km from the fault features may be a reasonable safeguard and may be enough to cut out the high intensity part of the ground motion, thereby permitting lower design forces, but in North-East India, even a distance of 60-70 kms may not be enough to substantially attenuate high intensity motion in an earthquake of magnitude 7.5 - 8.5 thereby necessitating provision for high seismic forces. Thus in an area of this type, where there will be no region without fault features within a radius of 60-70 kms, we cannot escape the severe assumption that the strongest earthquake could occur nearest to the site of the major structure from the known faults around. In other areas, the low probability of such an event can be taken advantage of in assuming that the strongest shock may not occur closest to the site.

The design for the ground motion generated by strongest probable earthquake from the nearest fault would naturally be very expensive and some compromise with the factor of safety has to be made without risking a disaster. In many structures it is possible to permit the stresses to develop to critical values and beyond to some extent when strongest earthquake is considered, with the provision, that for about half the size of the strongest motion no appreciable damage should occur. To a certain extent, this reduction factor is a function of the type of structure and it's importance. For example, the containment structure in a nuclear power plant, even in south India, could not be permitted this relaxation in spite of infrequent seismic events, but most other structures could be designed for half the extreme intensity or even less. In choosing this ratio, frequency of occurrence of earthquakes in the

61

region and the structural importance will be the controlling factors. Structures such as 'earth dams', if designed for the high earthquake forces, are extremely expensive, and sometimes not feasible. Their design for the ground motion generated by strongest probable earthquake from the nearest fault is seldom feasible and the designer has to accept a reasonable repairable damage in the event of the strongest shock.

It may not be out of place to mention here, the uncertainties in design inputs for structures like "earth dams". In their case, it is difficult to assume, with complete confidence, the damping the structure will offer to vibratory forces during an earthquake at any point of time since its value is strain-dependent. It is well known that damping is a major characteristic in changing the response of a system. Tests on earth dam models (with all their frailities) have indicated that the damping could vary from 2% to 30% depending upon strain along slipping planes. Between 2% to 30% damping, the amplification ratio of response could be in the range of 2 to 4. Thus accepting some damage i.e. slipping, and assuming high rate of damping in the extreme situation, safety against overtopping could be controlled without making the dam too expensive. For this set of conditions of design, even the strongest shock from the closest fault could be a reasonable assumption, but if we do not permit any slipping, considering only a fraction of the strongest ground motion appears to be adequate. Similar will be the position with rock-fill dams.

In concrete dams, the question that has to be answered is whether, in the case of maximum credible earthquake, cracking of the dam could be accepted. Concrete as a material has some energy absorbing capacity in the compression zone till it reaches high strain level, but in tension this level is very low i.e. practically no ductility. We have examined in the case of Koyna dam, which cracked in 1967, the effect of repeated earthquake occurrence with respect to the toppling over of the top cracked portion. We found that the oscillatory nature of earthquake motion does not cause leaning of the dam to an extent that it may over-turn. It does not, however, mean that we could permit cracking of a concrete dam. Even if toppling does not take place the crack will continue to extend and lead to other problems. Further, the very process of emptying the lake and repairing it, is expensive. This study, however, encourages us to permit the tensile stresses equal the cracking value in the event of a maximum credible earthquake. This gives a lot of relief in the design. Further, relief could be available by putting in richer concrete in tension zone so that the cracking value is higher. To give an idea of the extent of this relief, let us consider a concrete dam designed for a non-seismic zone. Its base will be about 3/4 of its height. In a seismic zone, the same section will stand reasonably well a uniform horizontal seismic force of 1/3 g if 500 p.s.i. tension could be permitted at critical sections. It may be mentioned that Koyna earthquake ground motion was approximately equivalent to 1/2 g uniform and, therefore, Koyna Dam section, which was not designed for earthquake, needed strengthening only to some extent with critical sections developing tension almost reaching cracking capacity.

In a seismic environment, a common question is, "what type of dam — concrete, masonry, earth or rock-fill — should be adopted" for a particular site. Concrete dams offer a level of confidence since, even on cracking, a disaster through sudden release of stored water is not likely to happen. The same is the position with masonry dams, although they are more vulnerable than concrete dams. In the case of earth and rock-fill dams, one feels insecure because a serious crack through the impermeable portion and slipping could lead to washing away of the dam with consequent disaster. The fact that no disaster has taken place so far due to an earthquake is reassuring although the number of strong earthquakes occurring in the vicinity of tall rock-fill dams so far is not large. It is, however, reasonable to think that pliability of earth and rock-fill will damp vibrations and accommodate off-setting to a great extent. Further, present day equipment and technology ensures considerable compaction and strength in such dams. All the same, one feels surer with concrete as material, if the foundation is competent enough to take additional load, inspite of the fact that concrete dams are stiff and have much lower damping ratio (2 to 10%) and are subject to much higher forces than earth and rock-fill dams, but it is also much stronger material and could stand higher forces. Further, earth and rock-fill dams absorb earthquake energy through subsidence and slipping, which are less amenable to analytical precision in view of the uncertainty in the values of elastic modulus, strength and density at various points in a highly heterogenous mass. These estimates for them are less certain than the estimates for stress in concrete dams.

I am leaving out the discussion for masonry dams, since I presume they will be built only where the probability of occurrence of strong ground motion is very low. I would suggest masonry dams for regions where the magnitude of shock is not likely to exceed 6 within 15-20 kms from them even once in their life time. There are hundreds of such low height dams in South and Central India standing for many centuries without any problem.

Incidentally, in India, in spite of our preference for concrete dams, we have to adopt rock-fill as the material for dams in severely seismic Himalayan regions since the foundation conditions at most places is unsatisfactory.

Effective Duration of Design Shock

Rock-fill dam design process has another judgmental decision involved and that is the "effective" duration of strong ground motion. It relates to the main shock and also to the foreshocks and aftershocks. For example, if an earth or rock-fill dam has been shaken to slipping and/or slumping during a shock, the subsequent shocks will go on adding to damage till repairs could be undertaken. In the earthquake of August 15, 1950 in North-East India, which was rated as magnitude 8.6 on the Richter Scale, there were 12 aftershocks of magnitude more than 6 in the first 24 hours after the main shock from the same spot, 23 more in the next 3 days within 60 kms to the main shock and 77 within a month in that region. Thus I would like to define "effective duration", for design purposes, to include also the aftershocks occurring within a reasonable period of time and within a reasonable distance, and work out total slumping and slipping for all of them to ensure safety against overtopping of dam or cracking of impermeable core. One has thus to assume with available data, the number of strong aftershocks likely to occur between the main shock and the time when repairs could be carried out. Data is scanty at most places and the above quoted shock may be exceptionally severe but ignoring aftershocks altogether would surely be unsafe.

In the past earthquakes, duration of the strong part of the ground motion has been observed as 5 to 15 seconds for magnitudes 6.0 to 7.0. For magnitude of 8.5 I guess, it may be about 30 seconds in the main shock. Aftershocks are generally smaller in size and strong motion content has smaller duration but their number is also more when the main shock has a high magnitude. Thus, unless specific data is available for a certain site, designing dams in moderate zones (M < 6.5) for 15 seconds duration of high intensity motion and increasing it to about 50 seconds in severe zones for M = 8.5 appears to be a reasonable estimate to include the effect of the aftershocks within about a month of the main shock.

The phenomenon of cumulative effects of strain can be quite a material consideration in ductile structures, where the strong part of the main shock takes the strain beyond yield. Subsequent peaks of the same event or those of the aftershocks later, can lead to collapse. In Arvin Tehachapi earthquake of magnitude 7.5 (July 1952) the buildings in the town of Bakersfield had little apparent damage, but many buildings which could not be repaired in time, collapsed a month later in an aftershock, which was of magnitude 5.8. Thus taking into account the effect of aftershocks, expected before repairs could be undertaken, is essential.

The construction of artificial accelerograms takes into account the size of expected shocks, their location, shape of spectrum expected, and the spectrum intensity indicating damage potential, but, at no stage, "effective duration" taking into account "aftershocks" plays a part. I feel it is an aspect which should be considered for design of major structures, expected to go non linear, in severe seismic environment. There is a need to collect data for whatever shocks it is available and to apply the laws of probability in estimating the "effective duration".

65

Frequency Content

One of the other problems that a designer faces while constructing an artificial accelerogram is the choice of natural frequency at which its spectrum should peak, since it is a function of the characteristics of the foundation material and to some extent those of the earthquake waves. If an accelerogram for the site is available, it makes the task somewhat easier, but even then the effect of the size of shock and the distance of its hypocenter could change the peak in frequency-from shock to shock. Most of the accelerograms, however, have their frequency content between 2 and 12 cycles per second, the higher values being recorded on harder foundations. Unless specific data for a site is available, it appears that 2 to 5 cycles for average alluvium, 4 to 8 cycles for medium rock and 7 to 12 cycles for hard rock deposits are good average estimates. The higher values in each range relate to shock originating from sources close by while the lower values for somewhat distant ones.

CONCLUSION

The above discussion regarding design accelerogram and its importance in severe seismic environment, when major structures are designed, only highlights the problems that designers face and have to make, quite often, difficult decisions based on experience and judgment of their own or their colleagues in the profession. In recent years there has been concentration of research effort more on the analytical studies of structures than on the collection and interpretation of data fed into the analysis. Further, data on studying motion relevant for the design of engineering structures is still not much in spite of intensification of effort in the last decade.

This brings me to the suggestion that some forum need be established to exchange information on the decisions and decision making processes for design of major projects in various seismic zones of the world. The International Association of Earthquake Engineering could play a role in it through publication of monographs on relevant and specific problems and projects. Earthquake is a phenomenon which we could not order at any site at any point of time. All other forces that engineers face could be reproduced or they repeat naturally quite often. Data collection in the case of earthquakes is a hit and miss process. Therefore an international agency could help pool the resources and information and reduce the uncertainties.

68

III. CLOSING CEREMONIES

Dr. Joseph Penzien presiding

July 27, 1984

Penzien - I am pleased to see so many of you have stayed for these Closing Ceremonies.

As many of you know, having attended previous World Conferences on Earthquake Engineering, the main purpose of the Closing Ceremonies is to formalize certain actions taken by the International Association for Earthquake Engineering. I should therefore like to turn the chair over to its President, Dr. Donald Hudson.

CLOSING CEREMONIES

BY

D. E. HUDSON, PAST-PRESIDENT, IAEE

Thank you, Professor Penzien. Fellow participants, ladies and gentlemen:

While you have been attending your technical sessions and other formal or informal meetings, the IAEE Executive Committee and the National Delegates have been very busy behind the scenes preparing an even more active future for the International Association for Earthquake Engineering. We have selected a site for the Ninth World Conference on Earthquake Engineering, we have elected new officers for the Association, and we have developed new initiatives for expanded programs. Before reporting briefly on these matters, I should like to introduce a number of people who have been of key importance to the development of IAEE. By this time in our Conference I am sure that they are well known to you. Professor Penzien you have already met, as well as our Secretary General, Dr. Y. Osawa, who I am happy to announce has agreed to continue in his very important position. I want to pay tribute here to the energy and devotion with which Dr. Osawa and his central office staff have handled our affairs, and to the support of the Japan Society for Earthquake Engineering Promotion which makes the central office possible. Next, I should like to introduce Professor Shunzo Okamoto, an IAEE

Director and Honorary Member, and then Professor Ray Clough, Consultative Member of the IAEE Executive Committee. We come next to Professor R. Yarar, a former Vice-President of IAEE, who organized the very successful Seventh World Conference on Earthquake Engineering in Istanbul, Turkey, in 1980. Professor Yarar was one of the initiators of IAEE, being a member of the Preparatory Committee led by Professor Muto which resulted in the formation of the IAEE.

I should like to mention at this point a man whom I would be introducing to you now, had he been able to be with us - Dr. John A. Blume. Dr. Blume is an Honorary Member of the IAEE, and a member of the Executive Committee. He is one of the primary organizers of the Earthquake Engineering Research Institute, our Host Organization here, and was a moving spirit behind the selection of San Francisco as the site for our present Conference. I am sure that you are all familiar with his many technical contributions to the field of earthquake engineering, in which he is one of the true pioneers. Dr. Blume has been unable to attend this Conference, in which he has played such an important role, because of a deep personal sorrow in his family, and we extend to him our heartfelt sympathy.

The remaining persons on the platform will be introduced as they appear in our program.

I have next the pleasure of announcing the place for the Ninth World Conference on Earthquake Engineering. At the meeting yesterday of the IAEE General Assembly of Delegates, the National Delegates accepted the invitation of Japan to hold the next Conference there. I should like to introduce the National Delegate from Japan, Professor Takuji Kobori, to extend to us all an invitation to attend the Ninth World Conference on Earthquake Engineering. Professor Kobori.

Remarks by Professor Kobori

President Dr. Hudson, ladies and gentlemen,

It is a great pleasure for me to address you on behalf of the Japanese National Committee on Earthquake Engineering.

The Japanese National Committee is privileged to announce that the Ninth World Conference is to be held in Japan in 1988.

We would like to welcome all of you, earthquake engineers and scientists, from all over the world to East Asia. We wish that you take this opportunity to visit not only Japan but also many other countries in East Asia, on your way to and on your way back from Japan. In this respect, we need cordial cooperation with our colleagues from East Asian countries.

We look forward with great anticipation to seeing all of you in Japan four years from now.

Let us renew our old and new acquaintances again, saying "Kon-nichiwa", "Hello" in Japanese. "Kon-nichiwa".

Thank you.

We now come to the announcement of our new IAEE officers for the period until the next World Conference. At the meeting yesterday the National Delegates elected the following eight persons as members of the Board of Directors: A. Lopez-Arroyo, Spain; J. Carmona, Argentina; L. Esteva, Mexico; G. Grandori, Italy; A.O. Hizon, Phillippines; J. Kuroiwa, Peru; T. Paulay, New Zealand; and J. Penzien, U.S.A. I have next the pleasure of introducing to you the man elected to be the new Executive Vice-President, Dr. Jakim Petrovski, of the Institute for Earthquake Engineering and Engineering Seismology, Skopje, Yugoslavia. Dr. Petrovski.

Our Statutes provide that when the Executive Vice-President is from a different country from the host country for the next World Conference, the IAEE President and the National Delegate from the host country can appoint an additional vice-president. This is our present situation, and I am happy to introduce to you now our new Vice-President, Professor Keizaburo Kubo, Professor Emeritus of the University of Tokyo, and Professor of Saitama University. Professor Kubo.

We come now to our highest office. As the new President of the International Association for Earthquake Engineering, the General Assembly of Delegates has elected a man with a long history of contributions to the Association. As a former Director and Executive Vice-

President, he is thoroughly familiar with our Association and is a person who we can with the utmost confidence expect to apply himself with diligence and effectiveness to our problems. It gives me great personal pleasure to introduce to you our new President, Dr. Hajime Umemura, Professor Emeritus of the University of Tokyo, and Professor of the Shibaura Institute of Technology. Dr. Umemura, will you please address a few words to the audience.

Umemura's remarks:

Mr. Chairman, Earthquake Engineers and Scientists, Ladies and Gentlemen,

It is my honor to be elected President of the International Association for Earthquake Engineering for the next four years.

First, I want to express my sincere gratitude to the hosting organization, Earthquake Engineering Research Institute, and the organizing committees and all individuals involved in preparing and executing this Eighth World Conference on Earthquake Engineering. The conference has been very successful in this beautiful city of San Francisco, and in this hotel of the proven earthquake resistance. We, all participants, enjoyed the cordial hospitality.

I want to thank Dr. Hudson for his excellent work as the President of the International Association for Earthquake Engineering for the past four years, the fruit of which we have just harvested.

Since the first World Conference in Berkeley, significant progresses have been observed in the area of earthquake engineering research and practices. At the same time, we learned bitter lessons from the natural punishments of earthquakes. We have learned that the application of some engineering can significantly reduce the earthquake hazards. Therefore, it is important to disseminate the research findings presented in the past and present world conferences, and to reflect them in practice as soon as possible.

My personal dream is that we can enjoy the game with earthquakes sometimes learning from earthquakes without any loss of human lives and properties and sometimes providing some defenses against earthquakes through research and code enforcement, rather than we look at an earthquake as a major natural hazard. I want to ride on an earthquake just like a

cable car in San Francisco. I need your deep cooperation to achieve my dream. Thank you, "Arigatou Gozaimashita"

We now come to another important action of the Executive Committee and the General Assembly of Delegates. Our Statutes provide that certain persons who have rendered signal service to the Association can be recognized as Honorary Members, upon nomination by the Executive Committee and confirmation by the General Assembly of Delegates. This honor has just been awarded to three persons, and I shall ask our Secretary General, Dr. Osawa, to introduce them to you.

Introductions by Dr. Osawa

Professor Rodrigo A. Flores, National Delegate of Chile, former Executive Vice-President, Organizer of the Fourth World Conference on Earthquake Engineering, Santiago, Chile.

Professor D. E. Hudson, Past-President, IAEE

Professor S. V. Poliakov, Central Research Institute of Building Structures, Moscow, Member IAEE Board of Directors

Since the Seventh World Conference on Earthquake Engineering our ranks have been thinned by the death of a number of our IAEE colleagues. I must report with deep regret the passing of: Mr. Otto Glogau, IAEE Director, and National Delegate of New Zealand; Dr. R.B. Matthiesen, IAEE Vice-President, and first Chairman of the 8WCEE Steering Committee; Dr. J.K. Minami, first IAEE Secretary General and Honorary Member; Professor N.M. Newmark, IAEE Honorary Member; Professor F.P. Müller, National Delegate of the Federal Republic of Germany; Professor A. Roussopoulos, National Delegate of Greece, active in the early development of IAEE - the father of the representative from Greece for this present Conference; Professor F.S. Shaw, National Delegate of Australia.

A final action of the Executive Committee and the General Assembly
of Delegates was the formulation and adoption of several short resolutions, which I shall now present to you:

I. The IAEE Executive Committee and the Assembly of National
    Delegates wish to express their great appreciation to the
    Host Organization, the Earthquake Engineering Research
    Institute, for the invitation to have the Eighth World
    Conference on Earthquake Engineering in San Francisco and
    to the 8WCEE Steering Committee for the excellent
    planning and execution of this highly successful event.

At this point I should like to read the names of the 8WCEE Steering
Committee members, who have worked so hard to make this Conference the
outstanding success which I am sure we all feel it to be. The Chairman,
of course, is Joseph Penzien, and the members are: M.S. Agbabian, A.K.
Chopra, N.C. Donovan, P.C. Jennings, R.G. Johnston, Christopher Rojahn,
H.C. Shah, Beverly Wyllie, and L.A. Wyllie, Jr. We all owe them a great
deal for their efforts.

Coming now to the next resolution:

II. The IAEE Executive Committee and the Assembly of National
     Delegates would like to express deep appreciation to Dr.
     Frank Press for the very thoughtful keynote address which
     he presented.

The third and last resolution grows out of a suggestion made by Dr.
Press in his keynote address:

III. The IAEE Executive Committee and the Assembly of National
     Delegates enthusiastically endorse the idea of an "Inter-
     national Decade for Natural Hazard Reduction" under the
     leadership of the international earthquake engineering

community, and recommend prompt action for implementation.

As you will see from this brief review of our IAEE activities, we may confidently expect a bright future for our Association and for steady progress towards our goal of preventing earthquakes from becoming disasters. I thank you all for your participation in our meeting, and will hope to see you all again four years hence at the Ninth World Conference on Earthquake Engineering in Japan.

I will at this point return the meeting to Professor Penzien.

Closing Remarks, Dr. Joseph Penzien

Ladies and Gentlemen:

We have now come to the end of a very successful conference.

For the success of the technical program, I wish to thank the authors, particularly the presenting authors, for their excellent contributions. The seven volume set of Proceedings will provide permanent documentation of their efforts.

I wish to thank all of you for your attendance and participation in the various Conference activities. Having found the Conference rewarding and fulfilling, we can all look forward with pleasure to the next World Conference on Earthquake Engineering to be held in Tokyo in 1988, where again earthquake engineering will be advanced and fellowship will be enjoyed.

I wish all of you a pleasant and safe journey home, and, as I now say good bye, I wish each of you good luck, good fortune, and good health.

I now declare this the Eighth World Conference on Earthquake Engineering closed. Thank you.

IV. STATUTES OF IAEE

82

STATUTES OF THE INTERNATIONAL ASSOCIATION

FOR EARTHQUAKE ENGINEERING

Including amendments approved by the General Assembly of Delegates at their meeting June 26, 1984 in San Francisco at the Eighth World Conference on Earthquake Engineering

* * * *

Art. 1   NAME

1-1   The name of this organization is "International Association for Earthquake Engineering" (hereinafter referred to as the "Association"). The initials IAEE may be used as the abbreviated name of the Association.

Art. 2   OBJECT

2-1   The object of the Association is to promote international cooperation among scientists and engineers in the field of earthquake engineering through interchange of knowledge, ideas, and results of research and practical experience.

2-2   The Association will accomplish its object by:

(a)   holding world conferences,

(b)   interchanging information, and

(c)   extending technical cooperation.

Art. 3   MEMBERSHIP

3-1   The Association is composed of National Organizations of Earthquake Engineering (defined in Art. 3-3, and hereinafter referred to an "National Organizations") approved for membership by the Executive Committee. The Executive Committee has

83

the right to terminate the membership of any National Organization by a two-thirds majority vote.

3-2 Individual members of affiliated National Organizations shall be deemed to be individual members of the Association.

3-3 A National Organization is composed of members, individual or corporate, accepted into membership according to the statutes of that particular organization. A member of the Association may belong to more than one National Organization, and these need not include that of his country of residence. A National Organization must have: (a) a Constitution or Statutes; (b) a President, Chairman, or equivalent executive officer; (c) a Secretary; and (d) an address for its secretariat. The total membership of a National Organization shall be not less than 8. Only one National Organization from a country shall become a member.

3-4 To become a member of the Association, an existing National Organization must send a letter to the Secretary General of the Association, signed by the Executive Officer and Secretary, formally applying for membership and indicating that if accepted the National Organization will do its best to further the object of the Association, to cooperate with it, to abide by its statutes, and enclosing; (a) its Constitution or Statutes; (b) the names of its current officers; (c) the address of the secretariat; and (d) the names of its current members.

3-5 Each National Organization shall designate a Delegate and a Deputy Delegate to represent it in the Association. There shall be only one Delegate and Deputy Delegate from each National Organization. The term of office of the Delegate and Deputy Delegate shall be four years, but reappointments can be made. National Delegates shall serve for not more than two successive terms.

Art. 4   ADMINISTRATION

    4-1   The authority of the Association shall be exercised through:

        (a)   The General Assembly of Delegates

        (b)   The Executive Committee

        (c)   The Officers

Art 5   GENERAL ASSEMBLY OF DELEGATES

    5-1   The General Assembly of Delegates shall be composed of all Delegates representing National Organizations affiliated with the Association. The Deputy Delegate shall represent the National Organization in the absence of the Delegate.

    5-2   The sessions of the General Assembly of Delegates shall be presided over by the President of the Association.

    5-3   The functions of the General Assembly of Delegates shall be:

        (a)   to elect a President, an Executive Vice-President, and Directors according to Art. 5-7;

        (b)   to confirm recommendations for Honorary Members of the Association;

        (c)   to approve the selection of the place of the next world conference according to Art. 5-8;

        (d)   to approve Association policies and procedures;

        (e)   to amend these Statutes according to Art. 11.

    5-4   A session of the General Assembly of Delegates shall be held during each world conference, at which time Officers and

Directors referred to in paragraph (a) of Art. 5-3 shall be elected. A quorum for a session of the General Assembly of Delegates shall be one-half of the National Delegates. Attendance at a session of the General Assembly of Delegates shall include: (a) National Delegates, who alone may vote; (b) Deputy National Delegates, with no voice or vote if the National Delegate is present; (c) members of the Executive Committee, with voice but no vote; and (d) other persons, with no vote, at the specific invitation of the President. If there is no quorum and the General Assembly meeting cannot be held, the business scheduled for the meeting shall be transacted by correspondence. In such a case it shall be the duty of the Secretary General to ensure that the elections to the Executive Committee are held through the post and that the process be completed within six months of the preceding world conference. In such an event, to save time, the formality of seconding names proposed by a Delegate as required in Art. 5-7 shall be waived. Further, in such a case the persons securing the highest number of votes shall be declared elected and the requirement of a majority of votes shall be waived.

5-5 At sessions of the General Assembly of Delegates, a majority vote of the Delegates present shall be required on all matters put to vote, unless otherwise provided for in the Statutes.

5-6 For matters requiring interim action by the General Assembly of Delegates, decision may be taken by postal ballot. This will require a majority of votes case for adoption, with the total vote cast at least half of the eligible votes, except as required by Art. 11-1.

5-7 The President shall appoint a nominating committee consisting of himself and two former elected Presidents or Executive Vice-Presidents not now serving in that office. This nominating committee shall submit to the Secretary General no later than one month prior to the session of the General Assembly of Delegates at the World Conference a slate of nominations approved by the Executive Committee consisting of one name each for the offices of President, Executive Vice-President, and eight Directors. Additional nominations for these offices may be made from the floor at the General Assembly of Delegates at the World Conference by any National Delegate present, to be seconded by another National Delegate. The candidate receiving a majority (more than one half of total votes) shall be elected. When more than two choices are available and none of the choices receives a majority of the votes on the first ballot count, that choice receiving the fewest votes shall be deleted, and a second ballot conducted. The procedures shall be repeated successively until one of the choices receives a majority of the votes. In the event of a tie vote for any office, the President shall cast the deciding ballot.

5-8 The General Assembly of Delegates shall select the place for the next World Conference from a list of candidate countries who have filed with the Secretary General a letter of invitation from the affiliated National Organization. If more than two choices are available and none of the choices receives a majority of the votes on a first ballot count, the choice receiving the fewest votes shall be deleted, and a second ballot conducted. This procedure shall be repeated successively until one the of choices receives a majority of the votes. In the event of a tie vote, the President shall case the deciding ballot. If at the time of the session of General Assembly of Delegates no valid invitations have been received, a quorum is not present, or a single candidate does not receive a majority, the Secretary General shall arrange for the location of the next World Conference by correspondence within a period of six months of the preceding World Conference.

Art. 6   EXECUTIVE COMMITTEE

6-1   The Executive Committee shall consist of the President, Executive Vice-President, other Vice-President, not more than eleven Directors, the Secretary General and Consultative Members. Eight Directors shall be elected by the General Assembly of Delegates and the three others shall be optionally selected by the Executive Committee, in order to improve the geographical distribution of the Directors. Not more than one Director shall be from one country. The past Presidents and Honorary Members shall be Consultative Members without vote. In addition the Executive Committee may co-opt any person suitable qualified as Consultative Member without vote.

6-2   The Secretary General shall be nominated by the National Organization of the country where the central office of the Association is located, and shall be confimed by the Executive Committee. The term of service of the Secretary General shall be at the pleasure of the Executive Committee, subject to reconfirmation at intervals not to exceed six years.

6-3   Not more than three members of the Executive Committee, minus the Consultative Members, shall be from any one country. When the Executive Vice-President is not from the country selected to hold the next world conference, the President, after consulting the National Delegate of the country, shall name an additional Vice-President from that country.

6-4   Officers and Directors referred to in paragraph (a) of Art. 5-3 shall be eligible for one re-election or reappointment to the same position.

6-5   The President shall be Chairman of the Executive Committee.

6-6　The functions of the Executive Committee shall be:

(a)　to transact the business of the Association in accordance with the decisions and policies approved by the General Assembly of Delegates;

(b)　to decide on admissions and withdrawals from the Association;

(c)　to assist the National Organization in the host country in the planning of the next world conference;

(d)　to make recommendations to the General Assembly of Delegates for its approval either in session or by postal ballot;

(e)　to fill any vacancy in the Officers that may occur between world conferences.

6-7　The Executive Committee shall meet during each world conference. During the interval between world conferences, the Executive Committee shall function through correspondence.

6-8　Voting of the Executive Committee shall take place according to the relevant provisions of Arts. 5-5, 5-6, and 11-1.

Art. 7　OFFICERS

7-1　Officers of the Association are:

President
Executive Vice-President
Vice-President, if provided by Art. 6-3
Secretary General

7-2   The functions of the President shall be:

   (a)   to preside at meetings of the Executive Committee and at
          sessions of the General Assembly of Delegates;

   (b)   to act on behalf of the Association in the conduct of
          the affairs of the Association in accordance with pol-
          icies and procedures approved by the General Assembly of
          Delegates.

7-3   The functions of the Executive Vice-President shall be to
       assume the duties of the President in case the President is
       unavailable.

7-4   The functions of the Secretary General shall be:

   (a)   to administer the central office of the Association;

   (b)   to maintain the records of the Association;

   (c)   to print and distribute publications of the Association;

   (d)   to keep in trust the money contributed to the Associa-
          tion and to provide an annual accounting of the Associa-
          tion funds;

   (e)   to receive the report of the nominating committee (Art.
          5-7) and invitations for World Conference location (Art.
          5-8)'

   (f)   to arrange for minutes of the session of the General
          Assembly of Delegates at the World Conference to be
          taken and distributed, including records of business
          transacted, movers and seconders of all motions,
          including nominations.

Art. 8   HONORARY MEMBERS

8-1   Honorary Members shall be selected on the basis of their distinguished service to earthquake engineering.

8-2   The executive Committee shall nominate Honorary Members, to be confirmed by the General Assembly of Delegates.

Art. 9   FINANCES

9-1   There shall be no dues nor assessments to member National Organizations of the Association.

9-2   Operating expenses of the central office of the Association shall be met by the National Organization of the country in which the central office is located.

9-3   Each National Organization shall be responsible for meeting its own expenses.

9-4   Expenses of a world conference shall be met by the host country.

9-5   The foregoing shall not preclude any member National Organization from voluntarily contributing to the funds of the Association or to the organizing expenses of a world conference.

Art. 10 GENERAL

10-1 The Central Office of the Association shall be located in the country determined by the Executive Committee.

10-2 The official language of the Association shall be English.

95

Art. 11 AMENDMENTS

11-1 Adoption of any amendment to the Statutes shall require two-thirds affirmative vote of the Delegates present at the Session of the General Assembly of Delegates; or two-thirds affirmative vote of the Delegates by postal ballot, provided the postal votes cast shall not be less than two-thirds of the eligible votes. No vote shall be taken on an amendment to the Statutes until at least three months have elapsed since the complete text of the proposed amendment has been distributed to the National Delegates.

V. MINUTES OF MEETINGS

98

MINUTES OF THE EXECUTIVE COMMITTEE MEETING OF IAEE

The Executive Committee meeting of IAEE was held on 24 July 1984 in
the Empire Room, Fairmont Hotel, San Francisco, the United States of
America from 3:00 p.m. to 5:00 p.m.

1. The meeting was opened and presided over by the President, Dr. D.E.
Hudson.

2. Those present were:

President:	D. E. Hudson
Executive Vice-President:	H. Umemura
Vice-President:	J. Penzien
Secretary General:	Y. Osawa
Directors:	A. S. Arya
	T. Boen
	J. Carmona
	A. Hizon
	J. Kuroiwa
	J. Petrovski
	J. Prince
	R. I. Skinner
Consultative Members:	G. W. Housner
	J. Krishna
	S. Okamoto
	E. Rosenblueth

3. Adoption of the Agenda

The agenda for the meeting was approved.

4. Report on 8WCEE by Steering Committee

Arrangements for 8WCEE was briefly reported by the Chairman of the Steering Committee and some of the critical issues related to the technical program, proceedings and registration were introduced for the future conferences. Since there were too many items to be discussed, it was agreed to form a sub-committee under the new Executive Committee and to discuss only most important items in this meeting to pass on to the Sub-Committee. There were some suggestions mainly on the item of "number of papers accepted for presentation."

5. Report by the President (Appendix I)

According to the document distributed to the members,, "IAEE President's Report for 8WCEE," the summary of IAEE activities since the 7WCEE in September 1980 was reported by the President. The following are the main items discussed and resolved during the meeting:

(a) Relations with other organizations
(b) Monograph Committee activities
(c) International Strong Motion Array Council
(d) Activities associated with 8WCEE
(e) Revision of the IAEE Statutes

6. Report by the Secretary General (Appendix II)

According to the document distributed to the members, "Report of the Secretary General," the brief report of IAEE Central Office activities was given by the Secretary General.

7. Subjects to be taken up at the General Assembly of Delegates on July 26, 1984.

101

7.1 Proposals to ammend the IAEE Statutes

Since sufficient time for consideration by National Delegates has been given of the proposed amendment of the IAEE Statutes, it was decided to put it for approval to the General Assembly.

7.2 Selection of place for the next World Conference

It was confirmed that Japan and the Philippines had submitted the formal invitation to hold the 9WCEE and that the selection should be made at the General Assembly.

7.3 Election of new Officers and Directors

The President explained the procedure taken by the Nominating Committee, which consisted of Housner, Hudson and Krishna, to nominate one name for President, one for Executive Vice-President, and eight for Directors and introduced following names:

President: H. Umemura
Executive Vice-President: J. Petrovski
Directors: J. Carmona

                                B. Chandra

                                L. Esteva

                                A. Hizon

                                T. Kobori

                                J. Kuroiwa

                                R. Park

                                J. Penzien

7.4 Central Office location

It was agreed to recommend to the General Assembly of Delegates the location of the Central Office of the Association in Tokyo, Japan as well as Y. Osawa as Secretary General.

7.5 Recommendation for Honorary members

It was agreed to nominate Prof. Rodrigo Flores, Prof. D.E. Hudson and Prof. S.V. Poliakov as Honorary members.

8. Other business

The proposed IAEE resolution I, II and III (see Appendix of the minutes of the Assembly of Delegates) were introduced by the President and approved by the members and it was agreed to introduce them at the Closing Ceremony after approval at the General Assembly.

APPENDIX I

Report of the President

This report will summarize briefly the activities of the IAEE since the Seventh World Conference on Earthquake Engineering in September 1980, as seen from the President's Office.

1. Relations with Other Organizations

The IAEE is playing an increasing role in the activities of a number of national and international organizations and is frequently called upon for official representation at meetings, conferences, etc., and to lend its name and support as a sponsor of various events. The IAEE is a corresponding member of the Liaison Committee of the International Associations for Civil Engineering, and is listed as an International Non-Governmental Organization under Category "B" - Information and Consultative Relations - with UNESCO. As examples of meetings at which the IAEE has been represented by the President, the Secretary General, or appointed members of the Executive Committee may be mentioned: Seventh European Conference on Earthquake Engineering, Athens, Greece, 1982; the 21st General Assembly of the International Association of Seismology and Physics of the Earth's Interior, London, Canada, 1981; Symposium on Earthquake Disaster Mitigation, Roorkee, India, 1981; Annual Meeting of the Indian Society of Earthquate Technology, Roorkee, India, 1981; 4th Session of the International Committee on Earthquake Risk, UNDRO and UNESCO, Paris, France, 1981; 5th Session of the International Committee on Earthquake Risk, UNDRO and UNESCO, Geneva, Switzerland, 1983; 2nd Seminar on Construction in Seismic Regions, UN Economic Commission for Europe, Lisbon, Portugal, 1981; Inauguration of new laboratories at the Institute of Earthquake Engineering and Engineering Seismology, University Kiril and Metodij, Skopje, Yugoslavia, 1981; International Conference on Recent Advances in Geotechnical Earthquake Engineering and Soil Dynamics, St. Louis, Missouri, 1981; 18th General Assembly of the International Union of Geodesy and Geophysics,

Hamburg, Germany, 1983; Annual Meeting of the Earthquake Engineering Research Institute, Pasadena, California, 1984.

2. Monograph Committee Activities

a.   The Monograph Committee on Seismic Zoning (G.W. Housner, convener) and the Committee on Non-Engineered Construction (A.S. Arya, convener) completed their work and the publication "Basic Concepts of Seismic Codes, Vol. I" was issued in 1981 by IAEE with the sponsorship of the Kajima Foundation. Arrangements were also made by the Indian Society of Earthquake Technology to reprint the section on Non-Engineered Construction and to distribute it widely in India. In view of the good reception which the monograph received at the 5th Session of the International Advisory Committee on Earthquake Risk, Dr. Arya is now reconstituting the Committee on Non-Engineered Construction with the aim of producing a revised edition including the results of recent research relevant to the practical aspects of such non-engineered construction. A meeting of the new committee is to be held during 8WCEE. The assistance of UNESCO with travel funds for the committee meetings resulting in the Vol. I monograph are much appreciated.

b.   Meetings of the Monograph Committee on Engineered Construction (J.F. Borges, convener) were held in Lisbon, Portugal in March 1981, and in London, Canada, in July 1981, along with a meeting of the monograph coordinating subcommittee. The draft of the Engineered Construction volume was presented in 1981 for discussion at the UN/ECE Seminar on Construction in Seismic Regions, where it received the general approval of the participants. After thorough review, the monograph "Basic Concepts of Seismic Codes, Vol. II, Engineered Construction" was published in 1982 by IAEE with the sponsorship of the Kajima Foundation. As for Vol. I, the work of the committee was made possible by travel grants from UNESCO.

3. International Strong Motion Array Council

In 1981 the IAEE Executive Committee approved the formation of an IAEE committee termed the "International Strong Motion Array Council",

under the chairmanship of Professor W.D. Iwan. The objectives as stated in the ISMAC By-laws are: (a) To establish general guidelines for array design and deployment; (b) To establish priorities for international arrays; (c) To facilitate the exchange of data obtained from strong motion arrays; and (d) To undertake special projects related to strong motion arrays as appropriate. To advance these objectives, three meetings have been convened since 7WCEE: London, Canada in 1981 in conjunction with the IASPEI General Assembly; Athens, Greece in 1982 at the time of 7ECEE; and Hamburg, Germany in 1983, along with the IUGG General Assembly. A further meeting is scheduled for San Francisco in 1984 during 8WCEE. The meetings have served a very useful purpose in bringing people together to discuss pressing problems of basic data collection, archiving, processing, and dissemination. ISMAC is now engaged in the preliminary planning for a sponsored "International Colloquim on Strong Motion Data Processing" which it is hoped can be convened soon after 8WCEE. The assistance of UNESCO with travel grants for the above meetings is much appreciated.

4. Activities Associated with 8WCEE

The following tasks related to the organization of the Eighth World Conference on Earthquake Engineering have traditionally been the responsibility of the IAEE President and Executive Committee:

(a) To receive abstracts of papers. For 8WCEE a total of 1,627 abstracts were received and acknowledged.

(b) To appoint reviewers. Three independent reviews of each abstract were obtained from an international panel of 36 reviewers appointed by the President. For each of the twelve conference topics, one reviewer was selected from the host country, and two from other countries. Countries represented were: Japan (7), India (4), Canada (3), New Zealand (3), Mexico (2), Turkey (2), Argentina, Peru, and Yugoslavia (1).

(c) To receive and coordinate the reviewers' decisions, and to provide an overall ranking to the 8WCEE Program Committee.

(d) To assist the 8WCEE Program Committee in the final selection of papers for presentation, and in the notification of authors.

An additional function of the IAEE President is to serve as a communications link between the 8WCEE Steering Committee and the IAEE Executive Committee and National Delegates. The 8WCEE is the first time that the IAEE President has been from the host country, and has had the opportunity to participate as a guest observer in the Steering Committee planning meetings. I should like to acknowledge here the great care with which the 8WCEE Steering Committee, under the chairmanship of our IAEE Vice-President, Professor Joseph Penzien, has at all times tried to accommodate in its planning the desires and hopes of the international earthquake engineering community to the fullest extent possible. As a guest at these planning sessions, the IAEE President, for his part, needed to be always aware that the overall responsibilities and hence the final decisions rested in the hands of the host country.

5. Revision of the IAEE Statutes

A number of small revisions of the IAEE Statutes have been made from time to time since their original adoption by the Preparatory Committee in 1962, but no comprehensive review of their overall appropriateness has been undertaken in recent years. In the course of responding to several specific suggestions for additional amendments, it appeared that this might be a good time for a more thorough review and revision, since there are at present no pending problems and no retroactive actions need to be contemplated. To this end, the President appointed a special subcommittee of the Executive Committee, consisting of G.W. Housner, D.E. Hudson, and J. Prince, to consider the basic question of revisions of the IAEE Statutes, and to prepare specific proposals for the Executive Committee if that appeared to be desirable. This committee consulted many people, and in particular received excellent help from Dr. Jai

Krishna, Dr. Y. Osawa, and from the late Dr. J.K. Minami, the first IAEE Secretary General, who was thoroughly familiar with the considerations leading to the original Statutes. After a detailed study of the Statutes, and a comparison with the Bylaws of similar international organizations, the committee circulated to the Executive Committee and the National Delegates some suggested amendments for their comment and discussion. Based on an excellent response from the Executive Committee and the National Delegates, which indicated a general agreement on many points and produced a number of constructive suggestions, the committee drew up a final draft which was again circulated. This final draft, which has had the benefit of an extended study, is now ready for referral to the Executive Committee for approval and to the National Delegates for final action.

6. The IAEE Headquarters Office

As IAEE activities continue to expand, we become more and more indebted to our colleagues of the Japan Society for Earthquake Engineering Promotion for the support of our headquarters office in Tokyo, and even more particularly to our Secretary General, Dr. Yutaka Osawa, for the time, skill and attention which he devotes to our affairs. Whether it is tending to a voluminous correspondence, negotiating contracts for travel grants, or representing IAEE at scientific and professional meetings in the far corners of the earth, Dr. Osawa carries out his duties with unfailing cheerfulness and efficiency. We all owe him an immense debt of gratitude, and we may express the selfish hope that he will continue for many years in this role that means so much to IAEE.

Among the projects traditionally carried out by our Japanese colleagues which have been of great importance to IAEE and to the field of earthquake engineering, we should call attention to the new edition in revised form of the publication "International Directory of Earthquake Engineering Research" which is now being completed. With the almost explosive growth of our field in recent years, this publication will be even more widely appreciated.

A second publication which the world awaits each four years is the updated "Earthquake Resistant Regulations – A World List". This has become the indispensable reference source for many of the practical details of earthquake resistant design which are so critical to the attainment of major IAEE objectives.

Another responsibility of the IAEE office has been to supply appropriate information on IAEE activities to the International Journal of Earthquake Engineering and Structural Dynamics. This bimonthly magazine published by John Wiley and Sons, Ltd., serves as the Journal of the IAEE. It is our hope that a page of IAEE news can become a regular feature of the magazine.

7. Executive Committee and National Delegates

Since the Seventh World Conference on Earthquake Engineering our ranks have been thinned by the death of a number of colleagues. We must report with deep regret the passing of: Mr. Otto Glogau, IAEE Director, and National Delegate from New Zealand; Dr. R.B. Matthiesen, IAEE Vice President, and first chairman of the 8WCEE Steering Committee; Dr. J.K. Minami, first IAEE Secretary General, and Honorary Member; Professor N.M. Newmark IAEE Honorary Member; Professor F.P. Müller, National Delegate of the Federal Republic of Germany, A. Roussopoulos, former National Delegate of Greece, active in the early development of IAEE, father of the representative from Greece for this present conference, and Professor F.S. Shaw, National Delegate of Australia.

8. Concluding Remarks

On a more personal note, I should like to express my own great appreciation for the opportunity I have had to participate in the affairs of the IAEE. The friendly cooperation which I have invariably received from everyone has made the experience an unmixed pleasure. My predecessors built soundly an effective and harmonious organization, and I hope that I have been able to maintain in some measure the strengths that they developed. My best wishes go with the Association as it moves ahead to an even more productive future.

Appendix II

REPORT OF THE SECRETARY GENERAL

1. General

The Seventh World Conference on Earthquake Engineering was held in Istanbul, Turkey during 10-14 September 1980 with about 750 people from 42 countries in participation. The Proceedings of 7WCEE were published in ten volumes by the Organizing Committee headed by Professor R. Yarar. The General Assembly of Delegates and the Executive Committee meetings of IAEE were also held in this period at the same place.

At these meetings the following Officers and Directors were elected and/or selected by National Delegates and Executive Committee members:

President	D. E. Hudson (U.S.A.)
Executive Vice-President	H. Umemura (Japan)
Directors	A. S. Arya (India)
	T. Boen (Indonesia)
	J. Carmona (Argentina)
	N. O. Henaku (Ghana)
	A. Hizon (Philippines)
	K. Kubo (Japan)
	J. Kuroiwa (Peru)
	A. I. Martemianov (USSR)
	J. Petrovski (Yugoslavia)
	J. Prince (Mexico)
	R. I. Skinner (New Zealand)

Dr. John A. Blume, Professor Jai Krishna and Professor Shunzo Okamoto were recommended by the Executive Committee to be an Honorary member of IAEE and the General Assembly of Delegates approved the recommendation unanimously.

The United States of America was selected as the host country for the 8WCEE at the General Assembly of Delegates.

During the period 1980-1984 the Association has functioned through correspondence and an informal executive Committee meeting. The main activities will be outlined in the following:

2. Memberships

There has been no country that became a new member. Columbia joined the IAEE in 1976, but the IAEE Central Office was not able to communicate with the national organization of Columbia at the time of 7WCEE in 1980. Just after the 7WCEE it became possible for the Central Office to communicate again with the Asociacion Colombiana de Ingenieria Sismica by the efforts of people concerned. This situation was informed to IAEE Executive Committee members and the membership of Columbia was affirmed.

At present, membership of IAEE consists of thirty-four countries which have appointed National Delegates and registered with the Central Office of IAEE. These countries are Argentina, Australia, Austria, Bulgaria, Canada, Chile, Colombia, El Salvador, Ethiopia, France, German Democratic Republic, Federal Republic of Germany, Ghana, Greece, India, Indonesia, Iran, Italy, Japan, Mexico, New Zealand, Nicaragua, Peru, Philippines, Portugal, Romania, Spain, Switzerland, Turkey, United Kingdom, Union of Soviet Socialist Republics, United States of America, Venezuela and Yugoslavia.

3. Revision of IAEE Statutes

The General Assembly of National Delegates held on 13 September 1980 in Istanbul unanimously approved the proposed revision of IAEE Statutes on Articles 5-3, 5-4, 5-7, 5-8 and 7-4.

4. Tasks Taken by the Association for the Period 1980-1984

a. International collaboration on formulating "Basic Concepts of Seismic Codes"

Since the Istanbul meeting, the IAEE published the Part I of the "Basic Concepts of Seismic Codes" in 1980 and the Part II, "Basic Concepts for the Development of Seismic Design Criteria of Engineered

Construction" in 1982, with a financial assistance from UNESCO for travel expenses of Committee members and from the Kajima Foundations for printing.

b. International planning of dense strong-motion seismographs arrays

According to the resolution of the Workshop on Strong Motion Earthquake Instrument Arrays held in 1978, the International Strong Motion Arrays Council (ISMAC) was formed by the Association in collaboration with the IASPEI. The Council members were appointed and the Bylaws were approved by postal ballot in 1981. After the 7WCEE The Council meetings were held in London, Canada in 1981, in Athens, Greece in 1982, and Hamburg, Federal Republic of Germany in 1983 with the financial assistance from UNESCO mostly for travel expenses of Council members. During these meetings the following items have been discussed:

- Catalog of Strong-Motion Data
- Worldwide Strong-Motion Data Processing, Archiving, Dissimination Center
- Reports of Array and Network Activity in Various Countries and Region
- International Colloguium on Strong-Motion Data Processing
- Director of Worldwide Strong-Notion Programs
- Rapid Communication of Strong-Motion Announcements

c. Others

The Central Office has gathered the information of other international organizations about how to collect membership fees, etc.

117

5. Publications

The following IAEE publications have been prepared and published:

- Earthquake Resistant Regulations - A World List 1984
- Directory for Earthquake Engineering Research, 1984
- Basic Concepts of Seismic Codes Vol. I and Vol II

6. Financial Report

The expenses to operation the Central Office in Tokyo since April 1980 were as follows:

April 1980 to March 1981	¥1,224,008
April 1981 to March 1982	¥1,389,816
April 1982 to March 1983	¥1,188,964
April 1983 to March 1984	¥1,247,428

The Japan Society for Earthquake Engineering Promotion has provided the funds necessary to operate the Central Office.

7. Others

The Central Office location changed from KKSK-NAKAJIMA Building (Shinjuku-ku) to the following address in December 1982:

KENCHIKU KAIKAN 4rd Floor
5-26-20, Shiba Minato-ku Tokyo 108, Japan

MINUTES OF THE GENERAL ASSEMBLY OF DELEGATES OF IAEE

The General Assembly of the International Association for Earthquake
Engineering was called to order by the President Dr. D.E. Hudson on July
26, 1984 at 2:30 p.m. in the Pavilion Room of the Fairmont Hotel in San
Francisco, California, the United States of America.

1. Twenty-seven (27) delegates from the following countries were
   recognized:

1.	Argentina	J. Carmona
2.	Australia	C.T.J. Bubb
3.	Austria	R. Grossmayer
4.	Canada	S.M. Uzumeri
5.	Chile	R. Flores
6.	Colombia	A. Espinosa
7.	France	J. Despeyroux
8.	Germany, Federal Republic of	G. Klein
9.	Ghana	N.O. Henaku
10.	Greece	A.A. Roussopoulos*
11.	India	L.S. Srivastava*
12.	Indonesia	T. Boen
13.	Italy	G. Grandori
14.	Japan	T. Kobori
15.	Mexico	L. Esteva
16.	New Zealand	R. Park
17.	Peru	J. Kuroiwa
18.	Philippines	A.L. Lazaro III
19.	Portugal	T. Duarte*
20.	Spain	A. Bernal
21.	Switzerland	J.P. Wolf*
22.	Turkey	R. Yarar
23.	United Kingdom	G.B. Warburton
24.	Union of Soviet Socialist Republics	G.S. Pereselenkov*

120

25.	United States of America	M.S. Agbabian
26.	Venezuela	A.E. Olivares
27.	Yugoslavia	D. Jurukovski

*   Authorized Deputy Delegates

2. The Agenda for the meeting was approved.

3. Report by the President

The President outlined his memorandum, main items of which are as follows:

(a) IAEE's role in the activities of national and international organizations

(b) A summary of committee activities for the Monograph Committee on Engineered Construction and the International Strong Motion Array Council

(c) Activities associated with the 8WCEE

(d) An outline of the revision of the IAEE Statutes

(e) Acknowledgement to the Japan Society for Earthquake Engineering Promotion for the support of Headquarters in Tokyo and to the Secretary General

4. Report by the Secretary General

The Secretary General presented the following items concerning the IAEE matters briefly.

(a) Officers and Directors elected and selected by National Delegates and Executive Committee members and Honorary

members confirmed by the General Assembly at the 7WCEE in
1980

(b) Report on IAEE Membership

(c) Revision of IAEE Statutes

(d) Tasks taken by the Association for the period 1980-84.

(e) Publications

(f) Financial Report

5. Amendment of the IAEE Statutes

The amendments of the IAEE Statutes were presented in a package form
and were approved unanimously.

6. Selection of Place for the Next World Conference

The delegate from Japan, T. Kobori, invited the 9WCEE to be held in
Japan, probably in Tokyo, and the delegate from the Philippines, A.L.
Lazaro III, invited the 9WCEE to be held in Manila, the Philippines. By
ballot of the National Delegates, Japan was selected as the host
country of 9WCEE.

7. Election of New Officers and Directors

(a) H. Umemura from Japan was unanimously elected President.

(b) J. Petrovski from Yugoslavia was unanimously elected
Executive Vice-President.

(c) For the offices of eight Directors a slate of nominations
was introduced by the Secretary General. Their names are:

J. Carmona, B. Chandra, L. Esteva, A. Hizon, T. Kobori, J. Kuroiwa, R. Park and J. Penzien. Out of the slate R. Park from New Zealand requested that his name be replaced by T. Paulay. The assembly was reminded by the National Delegate from Ghana, N. Henaku that there would be four Executive Committee members from Japan, if the new President would name an additional Vice-President from Japan, which would not be in compliance with the IAEE Statutes*. Subsequently T. Kobori from Japan suggested that his name be withdrawn out of the slate. The Chairman stated that the Nominating Committee concurred with the replacement and the withdrawal with the agreement of the Executive Committee members. Three persons were nominated from the floor: A.R. Chandrasekaran from India, G. Grandori form Italy, and A. Lopez-Arroyo from Spain. As a result of voting the following Directors were elected:

J. Carmona (Argentine)

L. Esteva (Mexico)

G. Grandori (Italy)

A. Hizon (Philippines)

J. Kuroiwa (Peru)

A. Lopez-Arroyo (Spain)

T. Paulay (New Zealand)

J. Penzien (U.S.A.)

(d) The location of the Central Office in Tokyo, Japan as well as Y. Osawa as Secretary General was accepted.

---

* Art. 6-3 Not more than three members of the Executive Committee, minus the Consultative Members, shall be from any one country. When the Executive Vice-President is not from the country selected to hold the next world conference, the President, after consulting the National Delegate of that country, shall name an additional Vice-President from that country.

124

8. Confirmation of recommendations for Honorary Members

The following Honorary members selected by the Executive Committee were introduced and approved by the Delegates:

Rodrigo Flores
D. E. Hudson
S. V. Poliakov

9. Other Business

(a) Three resolutions were read by the President and were accepted. (see Appendix).

(b) The Colombian delegate gave the following statement:

"First I should like to thank Dr. Osawa for his welcome back of the Colombian Association of Seismic Engineering to this Association. And secondly I would like first to propose a vote of thanks to Professor Hudson and second unanimous applause to Professor J. Penzien for his leadership of the Steering Committee of this Conference."

(c) The delegate from Canada made a suggestion on the procedure for election of new officers and directors toward the improvement for future Conferences. His suggestion was that it would be much more convenient for National Delegates to be informed at the beginning of the Conference of a slate of Directors suggested by the Nominating Committee so that they would be able to think about the additional nomination from the floor at the General Assembly.

IAEE RESOLUTIONS

I. The IAEE Executive Committee and the Assembly of National Delegates wish to express their great appreciation to the Host Organization, the Earthquake Engineering Research Institute, for the invitation to have the Eighth World Conference on Earthquake Engineering in San Francisco and to the 8WCEE Steering Committee for the excellent planning and execution of this highly successful event.

II. The Executive Committee and the Assembly of National Delegates would like to express deep appreciation to Dr. Frank Press for the very thoughtful keynote address which he presented at the Opening Ceremony of the 8WCEE.

III. The IAEE Executive Committee and the Assembly of National Delegates enthusiastically endorse the idea of an "International Decade for Natural Hazard Reduction" under the leadership of the international earthquake engineering community, and recommend prompt action for implementation.

MINUTES OF THE JOINT EXECUTIVE COMMITTEE MEETING OF IAEE

The joint meeting of old and new Executive Committee of IAEE was held at 17:30 hours on 27 July 1984 at the Empire Room, Fairmont Hotel in San Francisco, California, the United States of America.

1.   Those present were:

New Exec. Comm.	Consultative members	Old Exec. Comm.
President:	J. Krishna	President:
H. Umemura	E. Rosenblueth	D. E. Hudson
Exec. Vice-President		Exec. Vice-President
J. Petrovski		H. Umemura
Vice-President:		Vice-President:
K. Kubo		J. Penzien
Secretary General:		Secretary General:
Y. Osawa		Y. Osawa
Directors:		Directors:
J. Carmona		A. S. Arya
L. Esteva		T. Boen
G. Grandori		J. Carmona
A. Hizon		N. O. Henaku
J. Kuroiwa		A. Hizon
A. Lopez-Arroyo		K. Kubo
T. Paulay		J. Kuroiwa
J. Penzien		J. Petrovski
		J. Prince
		R. I. Skinner

128

2.   Introduction of the new President

   D.E. Hudson, the old President, introduced the new President, H. Umemura, and asked him to take the chair. Then, H. Umemura took the chair and conducted the meeting.

3.   Adoption of the Agenda

   The proposed Agenda of the meeting was adopted.

4.   Selection of board of Director members

   The following additional Directors were selected taking geographical distribution of the Directors into consideration:

   I. N. Burgman (U.S.S.R.)
   B. Chandra (India)
   M. Erdik (Turkey)

   Note: It should be noted that before the meeting the nomination of an additional Vice-President from Japan was already made by the President to be K. Kubo after having consulted with the Japanese National Delegate to IAEE according to the Article 6-3 of the IAEE Statutes. This was announced by Professor Hudson at the Closing Ceremony which was held before the meeting.

5.   Other business

   (a) It was agreed to form a Sub-Committee to consider the critical issues related to the technical program, proceedings and registration for future conferences and to appoint Professor Kubo to be the chairman and Professor Penzien and Professor Arya to be the member of that Committee.

   (b) Concerning the IAEE Resolution III, the idea of an "International Decade for Natural Hazard Reduction" suggested by Dr. Press in his speech, it was agreed to ask Professor Petrovski to take care of this item, and Professor Penzien promised to send a copy of Dr. Press' speech to be included in the Post-Conference Proceedings to the Secretary General to distribute it to the Executive Committee members for their further consideration.

(c) Dr. Krishna proposed to consider international cooperation for the items which he stressed in his Luncheon Speech during this Conference. This speech is to be included in the Post-Conference Proceedings.

VI. IAEE EXECUTIVE COMMITTEE MEMBERS AND NATIONAL DELEGATES

IAEE EXECUTIVE COMMITTEE MEMBERS
(After 8WCEE, San Francisco, 1984)

President	Professor Hajime Umemura
Executive Vice-President	Professor Jakim Petrovski
Vice-President	Professor Yutaka Osawa
Directors	Dr. I.N. Burgman
	Professor J. Carmona
	Professor B. Chandra
	Professor M. Erdik
	Professor L. Esteva
	Professor G. Grandori
	Dr. A. Hizon
	Professor J. Kuroiwa
	Dr. A. Lopez-Arroyo
	Professor T. Paulay
	Professor J. Penzien
Consultative member	Professor R. W. Clough
Honorary members	Professor J. A. Blume
	Professor R. Flores
	Professor G. W. Housner
	Professor D. E. Hudson
	Dr. Jai Krishna
	Dr. K. Muto
	Dr. S. Okamoto
	Professor S. V. Poliakov
	Mr. J. E. Rinne
	Professor E. Rosenblueth

IAEE NATIONAL DELEGATES

(As of 8WCEE, San Franicsco, 1984)

Argentina	Professor Juan S. Carmona
Australia	Mr. C.T.J. Bubb
Austria	Dr. Rudolf Grossmayer
Bulgaria	Professor Georgi Brankov
Canada	Professor S. M. Uzumeri
Chile	Professor Rodrigo Flores A.
Colombia	Dr. L. E. Garcia
El Salvador	Mr. J. Amaya G.
Ethiopa	Mr. Bekele Mekonnen
France	Mr. J. Despeyroux
Germany, Federal Republic of	Professor G. Klein
German Democratic Repubic	Dr. Peter Bormann
Ghana	Mr. N. O. Henaku
Greece	Professor Socratis S. Angelidis
India	Dr. Sri Pritam Singh
Indonesia	Mr. Teddy Boen
Iran	Mr. A. A. Moinfar
Italy	Professor Giuseppe Grandori
Japan	Professor Takuji Kobori
Mexico	Professor Luis Esteva
New Zealand	Professor Robert Park
Nicaragua	Dr. Armando Hernandez
Peru	Professor Julio Kuroiwa
Philippines	Dr. Angel L. Lazaro III
Portugal	Dr. Julio F. Borges
Romania	Dr. Gheorghe Serbanescu
Spain	Dr. Alberto Bernal
Switzerland	Dr. J. Studer
Turkey	Professor Rifat Yarar
Union of Soviet Socialist Republics	Professor G. S. Pereselenkov
United Kingdom	Professor G. B. Warburton
United States of America	Dr. Mihran S. Agbabian

Venezuela   Mr. Alberto E. Olivares
Yugoslavia   Professor Dimitar Jurukovski

VII. LIST OF ATTENDEES—8WCEE

LIST OF ATTENDEES

Country	Number of Registrants	Number of Acc. Persons	Number of Daily Reg.
Algeria	4		
Argentina	6		
Australia	5	2	1
Austria	5	1	
Belgium	4		
Bulgaria	1		
Canada	39	3	2
Chile	12	2	
China	28		
Colombia	5	3	
Dominican Republic	1		
Ecuador	1		
Egypt	2		
El Salvador	1		
Finland	2	1	
France	18	1	
Greece	5		
Guatemala	1		
Honduras	2		
Hong Kong	1		
Hungary	1		
Iceland	4	1	
India	20	1	
Indonesia	2		
Iran	3		
Iraq	1		
Israel	6	3	
Italy	74	8	
Japan	294	24	2
Jordan	2		
Kuwait	2	1	
Malaysia	2		
Mexico	27	3	
Morocco	1		
Netherlands	2		
New Zealand	23	7	
Nicaragua	1		
Norway	8	1	
Peru	8	1	1
Philippines	5		
Portugal	5		
Puerto Rico	5		
Romania	1		
Saudi Arabia	1		
Singapore	1		
South Africa	1		

Spain	4		
Sweden	2		
Switzerland	9	2	
Thailand	3		
Turkey	6	1	
U.S.A.	777	90	32
U.S.S.R.	6		
United Kingdom	21	4	
Venezuela	5	1	
West Germany	30	6	
West Indies	5	1	
Yugoslavia	17	3	
incomplete addresses	4		2

TOTAL NUMBER OF COUNTRIES:	60
TOTAL NUMBER OF REGISTRANTS:	1528
TOTAL NUMBER ACCOMPANYING:	171
TOTAL NUMBER OF DAILIES:	40

Algeria

Dr Amar Chaker
Controle Tech. De La Construction
Rue Kaddour Rahim Prologee
Hussein-Dey, Algiers

Mr D'Jamal El Foul
Controle Tech. De La Construction
Rue Kaddour Rahim Prologee
Hussein-Dey, Algiers

Mr M'Hamed Slimani
Controle Tech. De La Construction
Rue Kaddour Rahim Prologee
Hussein-Dey, Algiers

Mr Farouk Tebbal
Control Technique De La Const.
Rue Kaddour Rahim Prologee
Hussein-Dey, Algiers

Argentina

Mr Luis M Alvarez
ENACE S.A.
Av L.N. Alem 712
Buenos Aires   1001

Prof Juan Carmona
Institute Investigaciones Antisismic
Av Liberator S Martin 1290oeste5400
San Juan   5400

Mr Juan C Castano
Inpres
47 Roger Balet-Norte
San Juan   5400

Prof Luis D Decanini
Univ Nacional Cordoba
Cervantes 757
Cordoba, Cordoba   5000

Alejandro Giuliano
Inst Nat Prev Sismica
47 N Roger Balet
San Juan   5400

Prof Carlos A Prato
Nat Univ of Cordoba
San Eduardo 151
Cordoba   5014

Australia

Mr William H Boyce
Cameron McNamara Pty Ltd.
131 Leichhardt
Spring Hill, Queensland   4000

Mr Charles T Bubb
Australian Dept Housing & Constr
470 Northbourne Ave
Dickson, Canberra   2602

Mr. Ramesh Manandhar
Univ. of Melbourne
Dept. of Architecture
Parkville, Victoria   3052

Dr Peter J Moore
University of Melbourne
Department of Civil Engineering
Parkville, Victoria   3052

Mr Bevis G Smith
University of Western Australia

Nedlands, Western Australia   6009

Mr. Vaughan C Wesson
Phillip Inst. Tech.
Plenty Road
Bundoora, Victoria   3083

Austria

Mr. Emanuel Csorba
U.N. Development Org.
A-1400
Vienna

Prof Franz D Fischer
Univ. of Mining and Metallurgy
18, Franz Josef Strabe
Leoben   A - 8700

Mr Richard Fritze
Tech Univ of Veinna
Karlsplatz 13
Vienna   1040 Wien

Dr Rudolf L Grossmayer
OGE Austrian Assoc Equake Engr
c/o Sailerackerg 38-40
Vienna   A-1190

Prof Franz F Ziegler
Tech. Univ. Vienna-Aus.Soc. Ee
13 Karlsplatz
Vienna   A-1040

Belgium

Mr Patrick M Carels
Ontwerp & Advies Bureau Carels
Hundelgemsesteenweg 480
Merelbeke   9220

Mr Frederic M Henning
Tractionel
31 Rue de la Science
Brussels   1040

Dr Andre R Plumier
Univ of Liege
6, Puai Banning
Liege   B-4000

Dr Dionys A Van Gemert
K.U. Leuven Dpt Bouwkunde
2 De Croylaan
Heverlee, Leuven   3030

Bulgaria

Prof Georgi Brankov
Bulgarian Aca. of Sciences
17 November
Sofia

Canada

Prof Don L Anderson
Univ. of British Columbia
Civil Eng Dept. 2324 Main Mall
Vancouver, B.C.   V6T 1W5

Ms. Gail Atkinson
Earth Physics Branch
1 Observatory Cres
Ottawa, Ontario   K1A 0Y3

Dr Tarek S Aziz
Cvl Engr Dept McMaster Univ
1280 Main St West
Hamilton, Ontario   L8S 4L7

Mr Jean-Guy L Beliveau
Univ de Sherbrooke
Faculte des Sciences Appliquees
Sherbrooke, Quebec   J1K 2R1

Dr Yousef Bozorgnia
McMaster Univ.
Dept. of Civil Eng., McMaster Univ.
Hamilton, Ontario   L85 4L7

Prof Peter M Byrne
Univ. of British Columbia
Civil Engr. Dept. 2324 Main Mall
Vancouver, B.C.   V6T 1W5

Prof Sheldon Cherry
Univ. of British Columbia
Civil Engr. Dept. 2324 Main Mall
Vancouver, B.C.   V6T 1W5

Mr Charles G Duff
Atomic Energy Canada Ltd
Sheridan Park Research Com
Mississauga, Ontario L5K 1B2

Mr Mohamed T Elouali
Ecole Polytechnique
Cvl Eng Dpt Struct Div
Montreal, Quebec   H3C 3A7

Dr Antony G Gillies
Lakehead Univ
Civil Engr Dept, Oliver Rd
Thunder Bay, Ontario   P7B 5E1

Mr Cameron Kemp
Dominion Constr Co Ltd
3100 3 Bentall Cntr
Vancouver, B.C.   V7X 1B1

Mr Andrew W Metten
Bush Bohlman & Partners
#600-1500 W Georgia St
Vancouver, B.C.   V66 2Z6

Prof Milos Novak
Faculty of Engineering Science
The Univ of Western Ontario
London, Ontario   N6A 5B9

Prof Oscar A Pekau
Dept Civil Engr Concordia Univ
1455 Maisonneuve Blvd, W.
Montreal, Quebec   H3G 1M8

Prof Richard G Redwood
McGill Univ
817 Sherbrooke St West
Montreal, Quebec   H3A 2K6

Mr Brian T Rogers
Gulf Canada Resources Inc.
1124 Lake Sylvan Drive S.E.
Calgary, Alberta   T2J 2R1

M Saatcioglu
Univ of Toronto
35 St George St
Toronto, Ontario   M5S 1A4

A Scanlon
Univ of Alberta

Alberta

Dr Richard A Spencer
Univ. of British Columbia
Dept of Civil Engineering
Vancouver, B.C.   V6T 1W5

Mr Benedict H Fan
B.C. Hydro
Box 12121 555 West Hastings St.
Vancouver, B.C.   V6B 4T6

Dr Arthur C Heidebrecht
Mcmaster Univ
Faculty of Eng, Mcmaster Univ
Hamilton, Ontario   L8S 4L7

Mr Donald G Logan
Atomic Energy of Canada Ltd
34 Glendale Ave
Deep River, Ontario   K0J 1P0

Prof Noel D Nathan
Univ. of British Columbia
Civil Engr Dept. 2324 Main Mall
Vancouver, B.C.   V6T 1W5

Dr Avtar S Pall
The SNC Group
1, Complexe Desjardins
Montreal, Quebec   H5B 1C8

Dr Gerald Pernica
Nat Research Council
Division of Building Research
Ottawa, Ontario   K1A 0R6

Mr Russ Riffell
Genster Structures Ltd
P.O. Box 9520
Vancouver, B.C.   V6B 4G3

Dr Avigdor V Rutenberg
Dept. of Civil Engineering
McMaster University
Hamilton, Ontario   L854L7

George Salcudean
Atomic Energy Of Canada
157 Heath St
Ottawa, Ontario   K1H 5E6

Prof Arvind H Shah
Univ of Manitoba
Dpt Cvl Engr
Winnipeg, Manitoba   R3T 2N2

Dr Anne E Stevens
Earth Physics Branch, EMR
27 Carmichael Court
Kanata, Ontario   K2K 1K1

Dr. Siegfried F Stiemer
University of British Colombia
2324 Main Mall
Vancouver   V6T 1W5

Mr Alex K Tang
Northern Telecom Canada LTD.
8200 Dixie Rd. - Box 3000
Brampton, Ontario   L6V 2M6

Mr James H Tang
Ontario Hydro
700 University Ave H17
Toronto, Ontario   M5G 1X6

Mr Earle M Taylor
Ontario Hydro
700 University Ave
Toronto, Ontario   M5G 1X6

Mr Bernard Teper
Ontario Hydro
800 Kipling Avenue
Toronto, Ontario   M8Z 5S4

Mr Normand Thibeault
Ecole Polytechnique
6310 13 Ave. Rosemont
Montreal, Quebec   H1X2Y7

Prof John M Ting
Univ of Toronto
35 St George St
Toronto, Ontario   M5S 1A4

Prof Wai K Tso
McMaster Univ
Main Street West
Hamilton, Ontario   L85 4L7

Prof S M Uzumeri
Civil Engineering Dept.
Univ of Toronto
Toronto   M5S 1A4

Dr H R Woodhead
McKenzie Snowball Skallania
1510 Alberni St
Vancouver, B.C.   V6G 1A9

Dr Sheldon H Zemell
Fenco Engineers Inc.
33 Younge St.
Toronto, Ontario   M5E 1E7

Chile

Mr Hugo Barrera

Casilla 4792
Santiago

Mr Patricio Bonelli
Universidad T.F. Santa Maria
Casilla 110-V
Valparaiso

Prof Rodrigo A Flores
RFA Ingenieros LTD
Providencia 175
Santiago, Casilla   2895

Dr Pedro A Hidalgo
Universidad Catolica
Esc De Ing U Cat Casilla 114-D
Santiago

Prof Jorge A Jimenez
Fluor-Chile,S.A.
Casilla No. 16548
Santiago

Prof Carl S Luders
P.U. Catolica de Chile
Av. Vicuna Mackenna 4860
Santiago

Joaquin Monge
Dept De Ing Cvl U. De Chile
Blanco Encalada 2120
Santiago

Pedro Ortigosa
Idiem, U. of Chile
Plaza Ercilla 883
Santiago

Mancilla F Osorio
Socic Ing
Richard Neutra 876
Santiago

Prof Rodolfo G Saragoni
Univ of Chile
Avda Blanco Encalada 2120
Santiago

Prof Mauricio A Sarrazin
Univ of Chile
Reina Astrid 752 L.C.
Santiago

Dr Jorge Vasquez
Catholic Univ of Chile
Sch Eng Cath U Chile Casilla 114-D
Santiago

China

Ms Guanqing Chen
Pipeline Design & Research Ins

Langfang, Hobei

Mr Weimin Dong
Xing Hua Engr. Consul. Corp.
277 Wang Fu Jing St.
Beijing

Mr Sili Gong
Inst. of Earth. Engr. China Academy
Xian Huang Zhuang Rd.
An-Din-Men Gate, Beijing

Ms Ruikun Hao
Inst. of Build. Structure
Xian Huang Zhuang Road
Beijing

Mr Chingchang Hu
Beijing Institute of Arch. Design
Nan Li Shih Road
Beijing

Prof Yuxian Hu
Institute of Engineering
9 Xuefu Road
Harbin, Heilongjiang

Mr. Li Lee
C.R.I.B.&C.MMI PRC
No. 43 Xue Yuan Rd.
Beijing

Dr Huixian Liu
Inst. of Engineering Mechanics
9 Xuefu Road
Harbin, Heilongjiang

Mr Xihui Liu
Inst. of Earth. Engr. China Academy
Xian Huang Zhuang Road
An-Din-Men Gate, Beijing

Mr Li G Qing
Wuhan Building Materials Inst
Loshi Rd
Wuhan City

Prof Jumin Shen
Ministry Of Education, P.R. China
Quinghua Univ
Beijing

Prof Guang-yuan Wang
Harbin Arch & Civil Engr.
Dazhi Street
Harbin, Heilunjiang

Mr Qifa Xia
Water Cons. & Hydro Power Inst.
10 Chegongzhuang Xi Lu   Box 366
Beijing

Prof Haifan Xiang
Ministry Of Education, P.R. China
Tongji Univ
Shanghai

Prof Zhixin Xu
Tongji Univ

Shanghai

Mr Yaoxian Ye
Design Bureau, MURCEP
Bein-wan-zhuang Road
Beijing

China (cont)

Prof Daming Zhang
Seis Inst. of Guangdong Prov.
Seis Inst of Guangdong Prov
Guangzhou

Prof Guangdou Zhang
Tsinghua Univ
Pres. Office, Tsinghua Univ.
Peking

Prof Xue-Liang Zhang
Seismological Bur. of Jiangsu Prov.
3 Weigang
Nanjing

Mr Shurui Zhou
Xing Hua Engr. Consul Corp.
277 Wang Fu Jing St.
Beijing

Prof Bolong Zhu
Tongji Univ
1239 Siping Road
Shanghai

Mr Wei Zhu
Inst. of Eng. Mechancis
9 Xuefu Road,
Harbin, Heilongjiang

Mr Pao Hua Lee
Central Weather Bureau
64, Kung Yuan Road
Taipei, Taiwan   100

Dr Hue-Ming Liao
Eastern International Eng Inc
501 Tun Hua S. Rd. 11th Fl
Taipei, Taiwan

Prof Jeen-Shang Lin
Nat Taiwan Ins of Tech
43 Keelung Rd, Section 4
Taipei, Taiwan

Dr Chin-Hsiung Loh

Dept Cvl Engr Nat Central U
Chung-Li, Taiwan

Prof Sheng-taur Mau
National Taiwan University
Dept of Civil Eng Nat Taiwan Univ
Taipei, Taiwan   107

Prof Yi-Ben Tsai
Inst of Earth Sci Acad Sinica
POBx 23-59
Taipei, Taiwan   107

Colombia

Mr Alfonso Amezquita
Pontifcio Univ. Javeriana
Carrera 7a#40-62
Bogota D.E.   78-29

Mr Luis G Aycardi
Proyectistas Civiles
Apartado Aereo 21254
Bogota

Mr Augusto S Espinosa
Calle 86 No 20-21
Calle 86 No 20-21
Bogota

Dr L E Garcia
Assoc Colombiana de Ing Sismica
Apartado Aereo 4976
Bogota

Mr Luis R Prieto
Asoc. Colombiana De Ing. Sismico
Carrera 18A No. 8-06
Sogamoso, Boyaca

Ms Ana J Vargas
Asociacion Colombiana de Ing. Sismic
Carrera 49 NO. 86-10
Bogota D.E.   8

Costa Rica

Mr Jorge Gutierrez
Univ. of Costa Rica
Civil Eng. Dept.
San Jose

Ms Maria LaPorte
Univ of Costa Rica
POBX 764
San Jose   1000

Mr Jose Sandoval
Univ of San Jose Sch Cvl Engr

San Jose

Dr Franz Sauter
Franz Sauter & Assoc. S.A.
Apartado 6260
San Jose   1000

Ronald Steinvorth
Franz Sauter & Assoc. S.A.
Apartado 6260
San Jose   1000

Dominican Republic

Dr Dionisio Bernal
Dept of Public Works
Presidente Gonzales #2 Naco
Santo Domingo

Egypt

Mr Ahmed Hassanein
State for Tech Rsrch

Cairo

Dr. M. E Nassif
Cairo Univ.
Prof. Structural Eng.
Cairo

El Salvador

Mr Antonio G Magna
Ministry of Public Work

San Salvador

Ecuador

Otton Lara
Escuela Politecnica Litoral
Bx 7102
Guayaquil

Finland

Ms Kaya M Kainurinne-Supponen
Imatran Voima Oy
PO Bx 138
Helsinki 10   SF-00101

Dr Pentti E Varpasuo
Imatran Voima Oy
Malminkatu 16
Helsinki 10   SF-00101

France

Prof Denis P Aubry
Ecole Centrale Paris
Grande Voie Des Vignes
Chatenay-Malabry   92290

Mr Laurent Borsoi
Framatome
Tour Fiat Cedex 16
Paris   92084

Mr Patrice Cheron
Novatome
La Boursidiere RN 186
Le Plessis Robinson, Cedex   92357

Dr Jean-Marc Crepel
Ecole Centrale Paris
Lab Mec des sols Grnde Voie vignes
Chatenay-Malabry   92290

Mr Victor E Davidovici
SocoTec
"Les Quadrants"-3, Avenue Du Centre
St. Quentin en Yvelines   78184

Mr Jean Despeyroux
Consultant
1 Avenue Georges Clemenceau
Rueil-Malmaison   92500

Mr Pierre B Frisch
Commissariat a L'Energie Atomique
53 Rue Boucicaut
Fontenay-Aux-Roses   92260

Mr Philippe Maurel

1 Rue Herons St Quentin Yvlines
Cedex   78184

Mr Pierre A Sollogoub
Framatome & Co.
Tour Fiat Cedex 16
Paris   92084

Mr Jacques A Betbeder-Matibet
Electricite De France
Tour Edf-Gdf Cedex08
Paris   92080

Mr Marc Bouchon

1Rue Herons St Quentin Yvlines
Cedex   78184

Mr Jean-Francois Corte
Lab Central Des Ponts
BP 19
Bouguenais   44340

Mr Gabor Czitrom
Delegation Aux Risques Majeurs
25 Ave Charles Floquet
Paris   75700

Gilles Delfosse
CNRS/LMA
BP 71
Marseille, Cedex   13009

Mr Andre A Fleury
Stein Industrie
19 Avenue Morane Saulnier
BP 74, Velizy-Villacoublay   78141

Wolf Jalil
Socotec
3 Ave du Centre
78182 St Quentin en Yvelines   78182

Alain Pecker
Geodynamique et Struct
6 Rue Eugene Oudine
Paris   75013

Mr Jean-Paul Walter
Coyne et Bellier
5 Rue D'Heliopolis
Paris   75017

Greece

Mr. Stavros A Anagnostodoulos
IESEE
1 Hapsa
Thessaloniki   54250

John Drakopoulos
Greek Nat Org EQ Plnning Protect
196 Ippokzatous St
Athens

Prof Socratis Karydis
Athens Polytechnical Univ

Athens

Dr George C Manos
Univ of Thessaloniki
73 Mitropoleos
Thessaloniki

Alexandrus Roussopovlsoi
Greek Nat Org E-Quake Pln Prot
196 Ippokzatous St
Athens

Guatemala

Prof Hector Monzon
Landivar Univ.
Prof. School of Architecture
Guatemala City

Honduras

Dr Rafael Ferrera
Honduran College Cvl Engr

Dr Marco Zuniga
Univ of Honduras

Hong Kong

Te C Liauw
Univ Of Hong Kong
Dokfulam Rd

Hungary

Dr. Csak Bela
Technical Univ. of Budapest
Muegyetem Rakpart 3
Budapest   1111

Iceland

Pall Halldorsson
Meteor Off
Birstatarvugur 9
Reykjavik

Prof Edvar J Solnes

Univ of Iceland
Reykjavik   101

Mr Gudmundur Thorbjornsson
Linuhonnun, Consulting Eng.
Armuli 11
Reykjavik   105

Mr Helgi Valdimarsson
Almenna Verkfraedistofan H.F.
Fellsmuli 26
Reykjavik   105

Dr Anand S Arya
Univ of Roorkee
72/6 Civil Lines
Roorkee   247667

Mr. Arun Bapat
CWPRS
Central Water & Power Res. Sta.
Pune   411024

Dr Susanta Basu
E-quake Engr Dept
71/4 DS Barrack Govind Puri
Roorkee, U.P.   247667

Dr Brijesh Chandra
Dept of E-quake Engr U of Roorkee
207/1 Saraswati Kunj
Roorkee, U.P.   247667

Dr Anjur R Chandrasekaran

Univ of Roorkee
Roorkee, U.P.   247667

Murari L Gambhir
T.I.E.T. Patiala
Dpt Cvl Eng Thapar Eng College
Patiala, Punjab   147001

Dr Santosh Guha
U. of Poona
1056/c Shivajinaya Dhoke RJ
Puna, Maharaihra   411016

Dr Jai Krishna
Univ. of Roorkee
61 Civil Lines
Roorkee, U.P.   247667

GC Mathur
Nat Bld Organ
G Wing Nirman Bhawan
New Delhi

Navin C Nigam
Thapar Ins of Engr & Tech

Patiala   147001

Dr D K Paul
E-quake Engr Dept
133/2 Vikas Nagar U of Roorkee
Roorkee, U.P.   247667

D.K. Rakshit
Dept of Sci and Tech
Gvt India New Mehravli Rd
New Delhi

AR Santhakumar
Anna Univ
College Of Engr
Guindy, Madras, Tamil Nadu   600025

Dr. Suryya K Sarmah
Dept. of Environmental Science
Gauhati Univ.
Gauhati, Assam   781014

K Seetharamulu
IIT New Dehli
7 West Ave IIT Hauz Khas
New Dehli   110016

Mr Pritam Singh
Central Water Comm Govt of India
Sewa Bhavan, Ramakrishnapuram
New Delhi   110 066

Dr. H. N Srivastava

Mr Lakshman S Srivastava
Univ of Roorkee
Dept of E-quake Engr, U of Roorkee
Roorkee, UP   247667

Kumar J Sudhir
IIT Kanpur
Cvl Engr Dpt ITT
Kanpur   208016

Dr Shashi K Thakkar
Univ of Roorkee
Dept of Earthquake Engineering
Roorkee, U.P.   247667

Indonesia

Mr Teddy Boen
IAEE
Kmplx BDN O.12 Jln Ltjn S Prmn Slpi
Jakarta Barat

Mr Hinurimawan D Sudarbo
Indonesian Society of Earthquake Tec
JL. Setiabudhi II No. 21.
Jakarta Selatan   12910

Iran

Mr Heshmatollah Adibnazari
Earthquake Research Dept.
A.E.O.I. #7 Tandis Ave, Afrigha St.
Tehran

A Mohajer-Ashjai
Atomic Energy Org of Iran
No 34 Noubakht St Abbas Abad
Tehran   15338

Prof Madjid Sadegh-Azar
Univ Tehran
Univ Tehran Fac. of Engr
Tehran

Iraq

Dr Khalid J Fahmi
Bldg Rsrch Cnt Scien Rsch Cncl
PO BX 2136 Aliwiya
Baghdad

Israel

Dr Moshe Eisenberger
Technion
Dpt Cvl Engr
Technion City, Haifa   32000

Prof Sam Frydman
Technion-Israel Ins of Tech
Fac of Cvl Engr
Technion City, Haifa   32000

Prof Jacob Gluck
Technion
44 A. Einstein
Haifa

Dr E I Rosenthal
Israel Inst. of Technolog
Building Research Station
Technion City, Haifa   32000

David Yankelevsky
Cvl Engr Dpt
Technion City
Haifa   32000

Prof Joseph G Zeitlen
Israel Inst. of Tech.
Faculty of Civil Eng
Technion City, Haifa   32000

Italy

Dr Ugo A Andreaus
Istituto di Scienza delle Costruzion
18 Via Eudossiana
Rome   00184

Mr. Paolo Angeletti
Univ. of Rome
Via Eudossiana 18
Rome   00184

Prof Giuliano Augusti
Univ. Di Firenze
Facolta° Di Ing. Via Di S.Marta,3
Florence   50139

Dr Mauro Basili
E.N.E.A.
SP Anguillarese 301 PO Bx 2400
Rome   00100

Mr Raniero Berardi
ENEL-DCO
Via GB Martini m3
Rome   00198

Dr Franco Bettinali
ENEL
Via Ornato 90/14
Milan   20162

Mr. Vittorio Cagnetti
E.N.E.A.
Via Anguillarese KH 1, 300
Rome   00100

Ms Michele Candela
U.T.C. Comune D'Avellino
Via Tudro, 17
Avellino

Prof Fabio Casciati
Dept. of Structural Mechanics
Via Luino 12
Pavia   I-27100

Mr. Aldo Castoldi
ISMES
25 G. Cesare
Bergamo

Prof Vincenzo Ciampi
Univ. of Rome
Via Eudossiana 18
Rome   00184

Prof Alfredo Corsanego
Univ of Genova
Inst di Sci Delle Const ViaMont 1
Genoa   16145

Prof Georgio Croci
Rome Univ
Via Giulia 167
Rome   00100

Dr Alberto Basili
Nat Geophysical Inst
Via Ruggero Bonghi 11B
Rome   00184

Mr Albert Benuzzi
JRC-CEE

Ispra, Varese   21020

Dr Alberto Bernardini
Ist Costru Ponti Estrade
8 Via Marzolo
Padoua   35100

Mr Franco Braga
Univ of Roma
18 Via Eudo-Ins di Scien dlle Cons
Rome

Mr. Silvio Calvi

Via F.Filzi 7
Bergamo   24100

Prof Gianfranco Carrara
Univ. of Rome 'La Sapienza"
Dpt Tch Dll'Edizia Via Eudo 18
Rome   00184

Alberto Castellani
Politecnico Di Milano
P. Leonardo Da Vince 32
Milan   20133

Prof Giulio Ceradini

1 Largo Amba Aradam
Rome   00184

Dr Stefao Ciampicacigli
Aquilanti
Cassa, Meszzagiormo
Rome

Mr Giulio R Crespi
Italeco

Rome

Prof Salvatore D'Agostino
Univ. of Napoli
21, Via Claudio
Naples   80125

Mr Alessandro D'Amato
SV.E.I. S.P.A.
Via Poscolle N. 11
Udine   33100

Mr Alessandro De Stefano
Politecnico Torino
Corso Duca Degli Abruzzi 24
Torino   10129

Prof Andrea E Del Grosso
Univ of Genoa
1 Via Montallegro
Genoa   16145

Dr Ezio V Faccioli
Politecnico
32 Piazza Leonardo Da Vinci
Milano   20133

Prof Franco Focardi
Dip Ingegneria Civile
Via di S. Marta, 3
Florence   50139

Prof Renato Giannini
Univ of Rome
53 Via A. Gramsci
Rome   00197

Roberto Gori
Ist Di Sci Dlle Cons U. Padova
9 Via Marzolo
Padova   35100

Mr Massimo C Guidi
InstInstuto Sci e Tec Const
Via Antonio Gramsci, 53
Rome   00197

Dr Maurice Leggeri
Archstudio
175 Via F Baracca
Potenza   85100

Mr Michele Mele
Ist Sci e Tecn. Cost
Via Antonio Gramsci 53
Rome   00197

Dr Camillo Nuti
Univ of Rome
53 Via A. Gramsci
Rome   00197

Arch Mario A De Cunzo
Ministero Beni Cultural
1, Piazza Plebiscito-Palazzo Reale
Napoli   80100

Dr Renato DeAngelis
ENEA
48 Via Vitaliano Brancati
Rome   00144

Dr Mauro Dolce
Inst di Scienza dlle Construzioni
Via Eudossiana 18
Rome   00184

Dr. Pieralberto Fadalti
Achille Fadalti Costruzioni Spa
19, Antonini
Fontanafredda, Pordenone   33074

Carlo Gavarini
Universita Roma Fac. Ingegneria
Via Eudossiana 18
Rome   00184

Prof Antonino Giuffre
Univ of Rome
53 Via A. Gramsci
Rome   00197

Prof Giuseppe Grandori
Politecnico di Milano
32 Piazza Leonardo Da Vinci
Milan   20133

Dr Edoardo Iaccarino
ENEA
48 Via Vitaliano Brancati
Rome   00144

Angiolo Marroni
Provincia D Roma
Via 4 Novembre
Rome

Dr Claudio Modena
Inst. Construcioni, Ponti Estrade
V. Marzolo, 9
Padoua   35100

Mr Fabio Ortolani
Univ of Rome
53 Via A. Gramsci
Rome   00197

Prof Vincenzo Petrini
Politecnico Di Milano
32 P. Leonardo da Vinci
Milan   20133

Prof Palol E Pinto
Univ of Rome
53 Via A. Gramsci
Rome   00197

Dr Salvatore Pranzo
ENEA
48 Via Vitaliano Brancati
Rome   00144

Dr Giuseppe Rega
Instituto Scienza Delle Costruzioni
Monteluco-Roio
L'Aquila   67100

Dr Sergio Rossi
Aquilanti
Cassa, Mezzagiorno
Rome

Prof Francesco RussoSpena
Univ of Naples
c/ Stud Sparacio 49/F Piazzale Tech
Naples

Prof Guido N Sara
Dpt di Struct U. Della Calabria
Arcavacata di Rende
Rende, Cosenza

Dr Guiseppe Sferrazzo
Aquilanti
Cassa, Mezzagiorno
Rome

Dr Giovanni Solari
Univ of Genova
Inst di Sci Delle Cons Via Mont 1
Genoa   16145

Mr Silvio Tiano
Libero Professionista
Via Torino is. W
Messina   98100

Prof Fabrizio N Vestroni
Istitut di Scienza delle Costruzioni
Monteluco-Roio
L'Aquila   67100

Arch Adele Pezzullo
Ministero Beni Cultural
428 Via A. Falcone
Napoli   80100

Mr Antonino Pollicino
Libero Professionista
Viale della Liberta is. 517
Messina   98100

Roberto Puhali
Univ of Trieste
Piazzale Europa 1
Trieste   34100

Mr Masiani Renato
Univ Di Roma Fac Arch
53 Via A. Gramsci
Rome   00197

Prof Marcello Ruiscetti
Univ of Udine
Viale Ungheria 43
Udine   I-33100

Dr Tito Sano
ENEA
48 Via Vitaliano Brancati
Rome   00144

Mr Tremi P Sergio
Enel-DCO
Viole Regina Margherita m 137
Rome   00198

Armando Simonelli
Ins Tech Della Fondazione
21 Via Claudio
Naples   80125

Dr Maria C Spadea
Nat Geophysical Inst
11B Ruggero Bonghi
Rome   00184

Francesco F Valeri
Provincia Di Rome
Via 4 Novembre 119/A
Rome

Prof Giovanni Via
Univ of Rome
53 Via A. Gramsci
Rome   00197

Prof Carlo Viggiani
Univ. of Napoli
281 Posillipo
Napoli   80123

Capuro Vincenzo
Inst Tecnica Fond
21 Via Claudio
Naples   80125

Prof Edmondo Vitello
Politecnico Di Milano
32 p. Leonardo da Vinci
Milan   20133

Dr Alfonso Vulcano
Dip. Strutture Univ. Della Calabria
Via Crati 31/c
Rende (Cosenza)   87036

Dr Andrea Yignoli
Univ of Florence
3 Via Di S Marta
Firenze   50139

Prof Gaetano Zingone
Universita Di Palermo
Inst Sci Dlle Const-Vial Dlle Sci
Palermo, Sicily   90128

Japan

Mr Yashuiko Abe
Takenaka Komuten Co., Ltd.
2-5-14 Minamisuna
Koto-Ku, Tokyo   136

Mr Yoshihiko Akao
Ohsaki Research Institute/Shimizu Co
2-2-2, Uchisaiwai-cho
Chiyoda-ku, Tokyo   100

Dr Kinji Akino
Nuclear Power Enginneering Test Cntr
No 6-2, 3-Chome,Toranomon
Tokyo   105

Mr. Shimamoto Akira
Kobe Steel Ltd
1-Chome, Wakinohama-cho, Chuo-ku
Kobe   651

Dr Hiroshi Akiyama
Univ of Tokyo
Fac of Engr 2-11-16 Yoyoi
Bunkyo-ku, Tokyo   113

Prof Narioki Akiyama
Saitama Univ.
255 Shimo-Okubo
Urawa, Saitama   338

Prof Takashi Akiyoshi
Kumamoto University
2-39-1 Kurokami
Kumamoto   860

Mr Tadashi Annaka
Tokyo Elec Power Services Co, Ltd
4-6 Nishi-Shimbashi 1-Chome
Minato-Ku, Tokyo   105

Mr Takayuki Aoyagi
Tokyo Electric Power Services Co.
Hib. Chu. Bld 1-4 Uch-cho 2-chome
Chiyoda-ku, Tokyo   100

Prof Hiroyuki Aoyama
Univ. of Tokyo
4-2-13, Takatanobaba, Shin juku-ku
Tokyo   160

Mr. Kenichi Aragane
Chubu Electric Power Co.
Sakura Hamaoka-cho
Ogasa-gun, Shizuoka

Prof Takashi Arakawa
Muroran Institute of Technology
27-1 Mizumoto-cho
Muroran, Hokkaido   050

Mr Hideo Araki
Fclty of Engr Univ of Hiroshima
Shitami, Saijo-cho
Higashi, Hiroshima   724

Prof Akie Asada
Tohoku Institute of Technology
35-1 Yagiyamakasumi-cho
Sendai, Miyagi   982

Dr Yoshihisa Atobe
Waseda Univ
17-Kikuicho
Shinjuku-ku, Tokyo   162

Mr Naokune Endo
Toda Const Co, Ltd
171 Kyobashi, Chuo-ku
Tokyo

Dr Yasuyuki Esashi
C.R.I.O.E.P.I.
1646 Abiko
Abiko, Chiba

Mr C Fu
Disaster Prev Res Ins Kyoto Univ
Gokasho
Uji, Kyoto   611

Mr Katsuyoshi Fujiwara
Kobe University
Rokko dai Nada
Kobe   657

Prof Masami Fukuoka
Science Univ. of Tokyo
Chibaken 278
Noda, Chiba

Mr Nobuo Fukuwa
Ohsaki Research Institute
Fuk. Sei. Bld 2-2-2 Uch-cho, Chi-ku
Tokyo   100

Dr Kohei Furukawa
Faculty Of Eng. Yamaguchi Univ.
Tokiwadai 2557
Ube, Yamaguchi   755

Mr Yozo Goto
Ohbayashi-Gumi Ltd
4-640 Shimokiyoto,Kiyose-shi
Tokyo   204

Mr Ikuo Hama
Taisei Corp
25-1, Nishi-Shinjuku, 1-chome
Shinjuku-ku, Tokyo   160-91

Dr Takanori Harada
Public Work Inst. Technology
Asahi 1, Oaza
Ibaragi-ken   305

Mr Kyohei Baba
Engr and Rsrch Elect Pwr Dev Co
1-9-88 Chigasaki
Chigasaki   253

Dr Toneo Endo
Tokyo Metropolitan Univ.
2-1-1 Fukazawa, Setagaya-ku
Tokyo   158

Mr Jamshid Farjoodi
Inst of Ind Science Univ of Tokyo
22-1 Roppongi 7 Chome Minato-ku
Tokyo   106

Prof Yozo Fujino
Univ. of Tokyo, Dept. of Civil Eng.
7-3-1 Hongo, Bunkyo-ku
Tokyo   113

Prof Teizo Fujiwara
Disast. Prev. Res. Inst. Kyoto Univ.
Gokasho
Uji, Kyoto

Mr Toshibumi Fukuta
Blding Research Inst Minstry Constru
1 Tachihara
Oho, Tsukuba, Ibaragi   305

Dr Eiji Fukuzawa
Kajima Corporation
30 Flr Shin-Mit Bld 2-1-1 Nish-Shin
Tokyo   160

Prof Hisao Goto
School of Civil Eng., Kyoto Univ
Kyoto

Mr Yukiyoshi Goto
Kajima Corporation
30 Flr Shin-Mit Bld 2-1-1 Nish-Shin
Tokyo   160

Prof Masanori Hamada
Tokai Unev
1000 Orido
Shimizu, Shizuoka   424

Mr Mizuno Hatsukazu
Intl Inst Seism & E-quake Eng B.R.I.
1 Tatehara
Oho, Tsukuba, Ibaragi   305

Dr Satoshi Hayashi
Nikken Sekkei Ltd
11-11 Koraku 2-chome Bunkyo-ku
Tokyo   112

Prof Yoichi Higashi
Fclt of Tech, Tokyo Metro Univ
2-1-1 Fukasawa, Setagaya-ku
Tokyo   152

Yoshihiro Honda
Tec. Research Inst/Tokyu Const.co.
2-13-9 Miyazaki, Miyamae-ku
Kawasaki, Kanagawa   213

Dr Naohito Hori
Kokushikan University
Setagaya 4-28-1
Setagaya-ku, Tokyo   154

Dr Toshikatsu Ichinose
Nagoya Inst of Tech
Gokiso-cho
Showa-ku, Nagoya   466

Dr Michio Iguchi
Science Univ of Tokyo
Yamazaki Higashikameyama 2641
Noda, Chiba   278

Mr Toshikazu Ikemoto
Dpt of Const & Env Eng Kanazawa U
Kodatsuno 2-40-20
Kanazawa, Ishikawa   920

Dr Kojiro Irikura
Kyoto Univ
Disaster Prev. Research Inst.
Gokanosho, Uji, Kyoto   611

Yoshitata Ishikawa
Electric Pwr Dvlp Co Ltd
EPDC Chuoku Yaesu 1-8-17
Tokyo   103

Dr Yuji Ishiyama
IISEE, Bldg. Res. Inst.
1 Tatehara
Oho, Tsukuba, Ibaragi   305

Mr Satoshi Iwai
Junior College, Osaka Inst. of Tech.
16-1, Omiya 5 chome
Asahi-ku, Osaka   535

Prof Shibata Heki
Inst. of Ind. Sci. Univ of Tokyo
22-1 Roppongi 7, Minato-ku
Tokyo   106

Dr Toshiharu Hisatoku
Takenaka Komuten Co Ltd
27 4-chome Hom-machi Hgi-ku
Osaka   541

Mr Kojiro Hori
Osaka Gas Co., Ltd.
11-61, Torishima-5
Konohana, Osaka   554

Prof Masaru Hoshiya
Musashi Inst. Of Tech.
1-28 Tamazutsumi Setagaya-Ku
Tokyo

Prof Hirokazu Iemura
Kyoto Univ.
Dpt Cvl Eng Kyoto U. Yosh. Sakyoko
Kyoto   606

Mr Takeshi Iida
Sumitomo Metal Industries, Ltd.
16 Sunayama Hasaki-Machi
Kashimagun, Ibaragi   314-02

Mr Tetsuhiro Inohara
Nippon T&T Public Corp.
1-5-3, Ote-Machi, Chioyda-ku
Tokyo   100

Mr Kiyoshi Ishii
Ohsaki Research Institute/Shimizu Co
Fuk. Sei. Bld 2-2-2 Uch-cho, Chi-ku
Tokyo   100

Toshiko Ishiyama

                                   305

Dr Ryoji Isoyama
Japan Engineering Consultants
2-2-6 Okubo, Shinjuku-ku
Tokyo

Mr Yoshinori Iwasaki
Geo-Research Inst., Osaka Soil Test
1-8-4 Utsubo-Homachi
Nishi-ku, Osaka   550

Prof Osamu Joh
Hokkaido Univ
Kita-13 Nishi-8 Kitaku
Sapporo, Hokkaido   060

Mr Toshimi Kabeyasawa
Yokohama National Univ.
156 Tokiwadai, Hodogaya-ku
Yokohama   240

Yuko Kagami

4-2-8-5 Hanakawa Kita
Ishikari

Prof Hiroyuki Kameda
School of Civil Eng., Kyoto Univ.

Kyoto   606

Prof Makoto Kamiyama
Tohoku Inst. of Technology
35-1 Yagiyama-Kasumicho
Sendai   982

Dr Jun Kanda
University Of Tokyo, Dept. Archi.
1-3-7 Chome, Hongo, Bunkyo-Ku
Tokyo   113

Mr Ikuo Katayama
Tokyo Elec Power Services Co
4-6 Nshi-Shmbashi 1-Chome Minto-Ku
Tokyo   105

Prof Ben Kato
Univ. of Tokyo
Dept. of Architecture
7-3-1, Hongo,Bunkyo-ku

Mr Katsuyuki Kato
Institute of Industrial Science
7-22-1 Roppongi, Minato-ku
Tokyo   106

Dr Hiroshi Katukura
Tohoku Univ
Aoba Aramaki
Sendai, Miyagi   980

Dr Hideji Kawakami
Saitama Univ.
255 Shimo-Okubo
Urawa, Saitama   338

Mr Onose Jun-ichi
Tohoku Institute of Technology
35-1 Yagiyama-Kalumicho
Sendai   982

Dr Hiroshi Kagami
Hokkaido University
N13w8
Sapporo, Hokkaido   060

Mr Teruyasu Kamba
Kobe University
Rokkodai Nada
Kobe   657

Mr Takashi Kaminosono
Building Research Inst'
1 Tatehara
Oho-machi, Ibaragi   305

Dr Kiyoshi Kanai
Japan Univ Pruductive Eng Dept
1-2-1 Izumicho
Narashino, Chiba   275

Dr Yutaro Kaneko
Seibu Const. Co.,Ltd.
3-1-1 Higashi-ikebukuro
Toshima-ku, Tokyo

Prof Tsuneo Katayama
Inst of Ind Science Univ of Tokyo
7-22-1 Roppongi Minato-ku
Tokyo   106

Dr Daisuke Kato
Dept. of Arch, Univ. of Tokyo
7-3-1 Hongo, Bunkyou-ku
Tokyo   113

Kato Muneaki Kato
Japan Atomic Pwr Co
Ohtemachi 1-6-1 Chiyoda-ku
Tokyo   100

Dr. Fusayoshi Kawakami
Tohoku Univ.
2 Chome Katahira
Sendai, Miyagi   980

Dr Hiroshi Kawamura
Faculty of Eng., Kobe Univ.
Rokkodai, Nada
Kobe   657

Dr Akio Kawano
Kyushu University
6-10-1, Hakozaki, Higashiku
Fukuoka   812

Dr Kenji Kawano
Kagoshima U. Dept Marine and Cvl Eng
Gunmoto 1-21-40
Kagoshima-shi   890

Kazuhiko Kawashima
Pblc Wrks Rsrch Ins
Tsukuba Science City
Ibaraki   305

Sato Kazuhide
Sato Kogyo Co Ltd
47-3 Sanda
Atsugi, Kanagawa

Mr Kenji Kikuchi
Oita Univ
700 Dan-no-haru, Dept Arch. Eng.
Oita   870-11

Dr Yoshikazu Kitagawa
Building Research Institute
1 Tatehara, Oho-machi
Tsukuba, Ibaraki   305

Dr Ryosuke Kitamura
Dept. of Ocean Civil Eng., Kagoshima
1-21-40 Kourimoto
Kagoshima   890

Prof Hiroyoshi Kobayashi
Tokyo Institute of Technology
4259 Nagatsuta, Midori-ku
Yokohama   227

Prof Kazuo Kobayashi
Civil Engr Kyoto Univ
Yoshida-honmachi
Kyoto   606

Prof Takuji Kobori
Dept. of Architecure, Kyoto Univ.
Yoshida-honmachi, Sakyo-ku
Kyoto   606

Prof Kikuo Kotoda
Waseda Univ
17 Kikui-cho
Shinjuku-ku, Tokyo   162

Dr Kazuma Kawano
Chiyoda Chenical Eng & Const
3-1-4 Ikegami Shin Cho
Kawasaki, Kanagawa   210

Prof Masahiro Kawano
Dept. of Architecture, Kyoto Univ.
Yoshida-honmachi, Sakyo-ku
Kyoto   606

Prof Satour Kazama
Waseda Univ
17-Kikuicho
Shinjuku-Ku, Tokyo   162

Mr Hiromi Kihara
Struct Dept Nikken Sekki LTD
4-27 Koraku 1-chome
Bunkyo-ku, Tokyo   112

Nagata Kinji
Shizuoka Pref Govt
9-6 Oute-machi
Shizuoka

Mr Haruyuki Kitamura
Struct Dept, Nikken Sekki Ltd
4-27 Koraku 1-Chome
Bunkyo-ku, Tokyo   112

Mr Koji Kitazawa
Taisei Corp.
344-1 Nasemachi Totsuka-ku
Yokohama   245

Dr Katsumi Kobayashi
Tokyo Inst. of Technology
4259 Nagatsuta, Midori
Yokohama   227

Dr Masami Kobayashi
Kyoto Univ. Dept. Architecture
Yoshida, Sakyo-ku
Kyoto   606

Dr Isao Kohzu
Kyoto Univ. Faculty of Eng.
Yoshida Hon-cho, Sakyo-ku
Kyoto   606

Mr Yoshio Koyanagi
Ohsaki Research Institute
Fuk. Sei. Bld 2-2-2 Uch-cho, Chi-ku
Tokyo   100

Prof Keizaburo Kubo
Saitama University
255 Shimo-Okubo
Urawa, Saitama

Dr Kazuyoshi Kudo
Earthq. Res. Inst. Univ. of Tokyo
1-1-1 Yayoi, Bunkyo-ku
Tokyo   113

Prof Eiichi Kuribayashi
Toyohashi University of Tech.
1-1 Tempaku-cho
Toyohashi   440

Mr Naoki Kusano
Kajima Corp Cvl Engr Design Div
F 31 Shin Mits Bld 2-1-1 Nish-Shin
Shinjuku-ku, Tokyo   160

Dr Yoji Maeno
Cen Rsrch Inst of Elec Power Indus
1-6-1 Ohtemachi
Chiyoda-ku, Tokyo   100

Watabe Makato
U. of Tokyo
2-1 Fukazawa
Setagaya, Tokyo   158

Prof Minoru Makino
Kyushu Univ.
Dept. of Arch./Faculty of Eng.
Hakozaki, Fukuoka   812

Mr Miyajima Masakatsu
Kanazawa Univ.
2-40-20 Kodatsuno
Kanazawa, Ishikawa   920

Mr Kunihiko Matsubara
Chiyoda Chemical Eng & Construction
12-1 Tsurumichuo 2-Chome Tsurumi_Ku
Yokohama   230

Dr Mitsumasa Midorikawa
Building Research Institute
1 Tatehara, Oho-machi
Tsukuba, Ibaraki   305

Tadashi Mimachi
Waseda Univ
5-16-14-503 Minami Shinagawa
Tokyo, Shinagawa-ku

Prof Tetsuo Kubo
Nagoya Institute Of Technology
Dept. Arch. Gokiso-Cho, Showa-Ku
Nagoya   466

Dr Yoshio Kumagai
Inst of Soc-Eco Planning U. of Tsuku
Azuma 1-407-203
Sakura-mura, Ibaragi   305

Dr Kaoru Kusakabe
Kobe Univ. Fac. of Engr.
Rokko dai-cho, Nada-ku
Kobe   657

Dr Atsuhiko Machida
Saitama Univ.
255, Shimo-Okubo
Urawa, Saitama   338

Mr Masato Majima
Taisei Corp.
344-1, Nasemachi, Totsukaku
Yokohamo   245

Mr Yoji Makimoto
Mitsu Engineering & Shipbuilding Co.
1-1, Tama 3-Chome
Tamano, Okayama   706

Matsui Masaaki
Sho-Bond Const Co
34 Ichigayahonaiurachd
Shinjuku, Tokyo   162

Kaneko Masataka
Ohbayashi-Gumi Ltd
640 4-chome Shimokiyoto
Kiyose, Tokyo   204

Dr Chiaki Matsui
Kyushu Univ
6-10-1 Hakozaki Higashi-Ku
Fukuoka   812

Dr Saburoh Midorikawa
Tokyo Institute Of Technology
4259 Nagatsuta, Midori-Ku
Yokahama   227

Mr Koichi Minami
Osaka Institute of Technology
Omiya 5-16-1, Asahi-ku
Osaka

Prof Yamada Minoru
Kobe Univ.
Faculty of Eng., Dept of Arch.
Kobe, Japan   657

Prof Fusanori Miura
Yamaguchi University
Yamadai Oyama-syukusha B-302
Oyamakamimonaka, Ube   755

Mr Kaoru Mizukoshi
Muto Inst of Structural Mechanics In
30 Shjku Msi 211 Nshi-Shju Shju-Ku
Toyko   160

Prof Yoshinobu Mori
Nihon Univ.
62-4 Uneme
Koriyama, Fukushima   963

Prof Shosuke Morino
Dept. Architecture, Mie Univ.
Kamihama-cho
Tsu-city   514

Prof Koji Morita
Chiba University
1-33 Yayoi-cho
Chiba

Prof Hiroshi Muguruma
Kyoto Univ.
Yoshida Honmachi, Sakyoku
Kyoto   606

Prof Masaya Murakami
Chiba Univ
1-33 Yayoicho
Chiba   280

Yoshiteru Murosaki
Kobe Univ
18 Okazakitokuseicho Sakyo
Kyoto

Mr Hiroshi Mutsuyoshi
Saitama Univ.
255, Shimo-Okubo
Urawa, Saitama   338

Mr Toshio Nagashima
Takenaka Komuten Co., Ltd.
2-5-14 Minamisuna
Koto-ku, Tokyo   136

Mr Kazushige Mitsuishi
Kumagai Gumi Co., Ltd.
17-1, Tsukudo-cho, Shinijyuku-ku
Tokyo   162

Prof Koji Mizuhata
Faculty of Engr. Kobe University
Rokkodai-cho, Nada-ku
Kobe   657

Prof Shigeru Mochizuki
Musashi Inst. of Technology
1-28-1 Tamatsutsumi Setugaya-ku
Tokyo   154

Mr Mitsuo Morimoto
NTT Public Corp.
1-7-1, Hanabatake
Oho, Tsukuba, Ibaragi   305

Dr Takaki Morioka
Waseda Univ
17 Kikui-cho
Shinjuku-ku,Tokyo   162

Prof Shiro Morita
Dept. of Arch. Kyoto Univ.
Yoshida, Sakyo-ku
Kyoto   606

Mr Nobuyoshi Murai
Takenaka Technical Lab.
683 Hirao, Mihara-cho
Minamikawachi-gun, Osaka   587

Dr Suminao Murakami
Lab of Urban Safety Planning
4-5 Gobancho Chiyoda-ku
Tokyo   102

Dr Kiyoshi Muto
Muto Inst Struct Mech
Shinjuku Mitsui Bldg Rm3005
Shinjuku-ku, Tokyo

Prof Tomoya Nagasaka
Tokai Univ.
2-28-4
Tomigaya, Tokyo   151

Mr. Kinji Nagata
Sgizuoka Prefectural Government
9 - 6 Oute-machi
Sgizuoka-shi, Shizuoka Pref.   420

Prof Tomoyasu-Taguti Nakagawa
Konan Univ.
Okamoto, Higashinada
Kobe   658

Dr Masahiro Nakamura
Fujita Corp.
Otana-cho, Kohoku-ku
Yokohama   223

Prof Takeshi Nakamura
Disaster Pre. Res. Inst - Kyoto Univ
Gokasho
Uji, Kyoto   611

Mr Hidemori Narahashi
Kyushu Sangyo University
2-327 Matshka-dai, Higashi-Ku
Fukuoka   813

Mr Atsushi Ninomiya
Nippon Kokan K.K. Tech Res. Cntr
1-1 Minami-Watarida-Cho Kawasaki-Ku
Kawasaki   210

Prof Takao Nishikawa
Tokyo Metropolitan Univ.
2-23-5-410 Seki Machi-Minami
Nerima-ku, Tokyo

Mr Shigeru Noda
Kyoto Univ
Dpt Cvl Eng Kyoto U. Yosh. Sakyo-ku
Kyoto   606

Prof Sukeo O-hara
Yamaguchi Univ
Tokiwadai
Ube, Yamaguchi   755

Dr Hitomi Ohashi
Faculty of Engr. Hokkaido Univ.
N13, W8, Kitaku
Sapporo, Hokkaido   060

Dr Shintaro Ohba
Osaka Inst. of Technology
16-1 5 Chome Omiya Asahi-Ku
Osaka   535

Dr Izuru Ohkawa
Building Research Institute
Tatehara-1
Oh-ho-machi, Ibaraki   305

Mr Hachiro Nakamura
Disater Planning Kokubunji City Hal
1-6-1 Tokura
Kokubunji, Tokyo   185

Mr Susumu Nakamura
Sato Co, Ltd
47-3 Santa
Atsugi, Kanagawa   243-02

Dr Shinsuke Nakata
Bldg Research Inst
Tachihara 1, Ohho-machi
Tsukuba, Ibaragi   305

Nikken Sekkei Ltd
Nikken Sekkei Ltd
2-38 Yokobori Higashiku
Osaka   541

Mr Shuichi Nishihashi
Taisei Corporation
25-1 Nishi-Shinjuku 1-chome
Shinjuku-ku, Tokyo   160-91

Mr Hiromu Noda
Earth Science Institute
2004, Higashino-cho
Akaishi, Hyogo   673

Mr Masayoshi Notake
Mitsubishi Rsrch Inst
2-3-6 Otemachi
Chiyoda-ku, Tokyo   100

Mr Koichi Ohami
Faculty of Eng, Chiba University
1-33 Yayoi-cho
Chiba   260

Mr Yoshimitsu Ohashi
Dep Archit Fact Eng Univ Tokyo
7-3-1 Hongo
Bunkyo-ku, Tokyo   113

Mr Kenichi Ohi
Inst. of Industrial Sci.
Univ. of Tokyo, Roppongi 7-22-1
Minato-Ku, Tokyo   106

Prof Tatsuo Ohmachi
Tokyo Institute of Technology
4259 Nagatsuta, Midori-ku
Yokohama   227

Dr Yorihiko Ohsaki
Shimizu Construction Co.,LTD.
2-16-1 Kyobashi, Chuo
Tokyo   104

Mr Akira Ohtsuki
Shimizu Construction Co Ltd
Fuk. Sei. Bld 2-2-2 Uch-cho, Chi-ku
Tokyo   100

Mr Shin Okamoto
Bldg Rsrch Inst
1 Tatehara
Oho-machi, Ibaragi   305

Shunzo Okamoto
Ins Ind Sci
7-22-1 Roppongi Minato-ku
Tokyo   106

Prof Syun'itiro Omote
Kyushu Sangyo Univ
2-327 Syokadai Higashi-ku
Fukuoka   813

Prof Shunsuke Otani
Univ. of Tokyo
4-21-22-106 Hamadayama, Suginami-ku
Tokyo   168

Prof Masakazu Ozaki
Chiva Univ.
1-33 Yayio-cho
Chiba   260

Dr Motoo Saisho
Kumamoto Univ
2-39-1 Kurokami
Kumamoto   860

Mr Nobuo Sakaguchi
Shimizu Construction Co. Ltd.
4-17 Etchujima 3-chome, Koto-ku
Tokyo   135

Mr Isao Sakamoto
Tokyo University
7-3-1 Hongo
Bunkyo-ku, Tokyo

Mr Fumio Sasaki
Kajima Corporation
2-7, Motoakasaka, 1-chome
Minato-ku, Tokyo   107

Prof Yutaka Ohta
Faculty of Engr. Hokkaido Univ.
N13,W8 Kita-ku
Sapporo, Hokkaido   060

Dr Shigeyuki Okada
Hokkaido University
N13 W8
Sapporo, Hokkaido   060

Prof Shunzo Okamoto
Institute of Industrial Science
7-22-1 Roppongi, Minato-ku
Tokyo   106

Mr Mitsuo Okumura
Kozo Keikaku Engr Inc
4-38-13 Honcho Nakano-ku
Tokyo

Prof Yutaka Osawa
E.R.I. University of Tokyo
1-1-1 Yayoi, Bunkyo-ku
Tokyo   113

Mr Yukio Otsuki
Shimizu Construction Co., LTD.
16-1 Kyobashi 2 chome
Tokyo   104

Dr Osamu Saijo
Nihon Univ.
Dept Mar. Arch & Eng.Col. Sci & Tch
Tokyo   101

Yukio Saito
Nikken Sekkei Ltd
2-38 Yokobori Higashi-ku
Osaka   541

Mr Fujikazu Sakai
Kawasaki Heavy Ind
2-4-25, Minamisuna,Koto-Ku
Tokyo   136

Mr Takanori Samano
Tokyo Institute Of Technology
4259 Nagatsuta, Midori-Ku
Yokahama   227

Dr Tadanobu Sato
D.P.R.I. Kyoto Univ.
Gokasho
Uji, Kyoto   611

Mr Takao Sato
Meiho Eng. Ltd.
6-25-11 ,Gotanda Shinagawa
Tokyo

Mr Matsutaro Seki
Tech Rsrch Inst Ohbayashi-Gumi,Ltd
4-640 Shimokiyoto
Kiyose-Shi, Tokyo   204

Prof Kazuoh Seo
Tokyo Institute Of Technology
4259 Nagatsuta, Midori-Ku
Yokohama   227

Prof Akenori Shibata
Tohoku Univ.
Aramaki Aoba
Sendai   980

Mr Mitsuru Shibusawa
Chiyoda Chemical Eng & Const.
3-1-4, Ikegami Shin Cho
Kawasaki, Kanagawa   210

Ochiai Shiger
Chiyoda Chemical
1-12-1 Tsurum-Chou Tsurumieu
Yokohama   231

Mr Katsumi Shimizu
Res.Inst.Shimizu Const. Co.
4-17 Etchuiima 3-Chome Koto-ku
Tokyo   135

Dr Yasushi Shimizu
Fclt of Tech, Tokyo Metro Univ
2-1-1 Fukasawa, Setagaya-ku
Tokyo   152

Mr Izumi Shino
Inst of Ind Science Univ of Tokyo
7-22-1 Roppongi, Minato-ku
Tokyo   106

Dr Keishi Shiono
Tokyo Metropolitan Univ.
1-1 Fukasawa 2-chome
Setagaya-ku, Tokyo   158

Mr Hideo Suitsu
Nikken Sekkei Ltd
4-27 Koraku 1-chome
Bunkyo-ku, Tokyo   112

Mr Tsuyoshi Sawahashi
NTT Public Corp
1-7-1 Hanabatake
Oho-cho, Tsukuba, Ibaragi   305

Mr Koji Sekiguchi
Tech. Res. Cntr. ,Nippon Kokan
1-1 Minamiwatarida-cho, Kawasaki-ku
Kawasaki   210

Prof Harvey A Shapiro
Osaka Geijutsu Univ
Kumano Shokuin Shukusha, 136
Kyoto   606

Dr Michio Shibata
Osaka Institute of Technology
Omiya 5-16-1 Asahi-ku
Osaka

Prof Toshio Shiga
Tohoku Univ.
Aramaki Aoba
Sendai   980

Prof Etsuzo Shima
Equake Rsrch Inst Univ of Toyko
1-1-1 Yayoi
Bunkyo-ku, Tokyo   113

Dr Nobuyuki Shimizu
Chiyoda Chemical Eng. & Const.
3-1-4 Ikegami Shin Cho
Kawasaki, Kanagawa   210

Mr Ikuo Shimoda
Oiles Indus Co Ltd
8 Kirihara-cho
Fujisawa, Kanagawa   252

Mr Hiroo Shiojiri
Cen Rsrch Inst of Elec Power Industr
1646 Abiko Abiko-shi
Chiba   270-11

Dr Shunsuke Sugano
Takenaka Tech Resh Lab
2-5-14 Minamisuna, Koto-ku
Tokyo   136

Hiroyuki Suzuki
Univ of Tsukuba
Sakura,Niihari
Ibaraki   305

Prof Kohei Suzuki
Tokyo Metropolitan University
2-1-1 Fukazawa Setagaya-Ku
Tokyo   158

Dr Yasunori Suzuki
Geophys Inst Fac Sci Toyko Univ
Yayoi 2-11-16, Bunkyo ku
Tokyo   113

Dr Sugano Tadashi
Kajima Corporation
30 Flr Shin-Mit Bld 2-1-1 Nish-Shin
Tokyo   160

Prof Hiroshi Tajimi
College of Sci. & Tech.
Nihon U Sur. Kanda, Chiyoda-ku
Tokyo   101

Prof Shiro Takada
Dept. of Civil Eng., Kobe Univ.

Rokkodai, Kobe   657

Mr Katsuya Takahashi
Kajima Inst. of Const. Tech.
19-1,2-chome, Tobitakyu
Chofu, Tokyo   182

Enomoto Takahisa
Kanagawa Univ
3-27-1 Rokkakubashi Kokoku-ku
Yokohama   221

Mr Tomiya Takatani
Kobe Univ
Dept. of Civil Eng.
Rokkokai, Kobe   657

Dr Toshikazu Takeda
Tech Rsrch Inst Ohbayashi-Gumi Ltd
4-640 Shimokiyoto
Kiyose-Shi, Tokyo   204

Mr Yasuo Takenaka
Kajima Corporation
30 Flr Shin-Mit Bld 2-1-1 Nish-Shin
Tokyo   160

Mr Mitsugu Takita
Hachinohe Inst of Tech
88-1 Oobiraki, Myou-aza, Ooaza
Hachinohe-shi, Aomori   031

Dr Norio Suzuki
Kajima Corporation
30 Flr Shin-Mit Bld 2-1-1 Nish-Shin
Tokyo   160

Mr Mototsugu Tabuchi
Kobe University
Rokkodai, Nada
Kobe   657

Mr Yasuhisa Tagawa
Yokohama Nat Univ
156 Tokiwadai Hodogaya-ku
Yokohama   240

Mr Akira Takada
Oiles Indus Co Ltd
3-2 Shiba-Daimon 1-chome
Minato-ku, Tokyo   105

Mr Junichi Takahashi
Tohoku Univ.
Aramaki Aoba
Sendai   980

Kunil Takahiro
Tokyo Metro Univ
2-1-1 Fukazawa-tyo
Setagaya-ku, Tokyo

Prof Koichi Takanashi
Inst. of Industrial Sci.
Univ. of Tokyo Roppongi 7-22-1
Minato-ku, Tokyo   106

Prof Jin-Ichi Takeda
Kumamoto Institute of Technology
4-22-1
Ikeda, Kumamoto   860

Prof Hirokazu Takemiya
Okayama Univ Dept Civil Eng
Tsushima Naka 3-1-1
Okayama   700

Prof Katsuki Takiguchi
Nagoya Inst of Tech
Gokiso-cho, Showa-ku
Nagoya   466

Prof Haruo Takizawa
Hokkaido Univ
Eng. Hokkaido Univ N-13,W-8,Kita-ku
Sapporo, Hokkaido   060

Prof Choshiro Tamura
Institute of Industrial Science
U. of Tokyo 7-22-1 Roppongo
Minato-ku, Tokyo   106

Dr Teiji Tanaka
Ohsaki Research Institute/Shimizu Co
Fuk. Sei. Bld 2-2-2 Uch-cho, Chi-ku
Tokyo   100

Prof Yasuo Tanaka
Waseda Univ.
3-4-1 Okubo Shinjuku
Tokyo

Dr Hidetake Taniguchi
Ohbayashi-Gumi, Ltd
3,2-Chome Kanda Tsukasa-cho
Chiyoda-ku,Tokyo

Prof Kenzo Toki
Kyoto Univ
Gokasho
Uji, Kyoto   611

Mr Kosuke Tomita
Hazama-Gumi, Ltd.
2-5-8 Kita-Aoyama Minato-ku
Tokyo   107

Mr. Toshio Toritani
Toda Construction Co., Ltd.
209 Kamihongo
Matsudo-shi, Chiba

Mr Iwamoto Toshiyuki
Kubota, Ltd
2-26 Ohama-cho
Amagasaki, Hyogo   660

Mr Keigo Tsuda
Kyushu University
6-10-1, Hakozaki Higashe-ku
Fukuoka   812

Mr Mitsuru Tsujita
Hazama-Gumi,Ltd.
17-23,Honmachi-Nishi 4-chome
Yono, Saitama   338

Mr Kozo Tsumura
Fclt of Tech Tokyo Metro Univ
2-1-1 Fukasawa, Setagaya-ku
Tokyo   152

Mr Naoki Tanaka
Kajima Inst. of Const. Tech.
19-1,2-chome, Tobitakyu
Chofu, Tokyo   182

Mr Tsutomu Tanaka
Oriental Consultants Co.
1-17-1 Shibuya
Shibuya-ku, Tokyo   150

Prof Sukenobu Tani
Dept. Of Arch. Waseda Univ.
3-4-1 Okubo Shinjuko-Ku
Tokyo   160

Mr Takashi Tazoh
Shimizu Const. Co.,Ltd.
4-17, Etchujima 3-chome
Koto-ku, Tokyo   135

Prof Masahide Tomii
Kyushu Univ.
12-1 Nagazumi 5-chome Minami-ku
Fukuoka   815

Dr Minoru Tomizawa
Science Univ of Tokyo
Yamazaki Higashikameyama 2641
Noda, Chiba   278

Toritani Toshio
Toda Cons Co Ltd
209 Kamihongo
Matsudo-shi, Chiba

Mr Hiroaki Tsubokawa
Fire & Marine Ins. Rating Assoc
2-9 Awaji-cho, Kanda
Chiyoda-ku, Tokyo   100

Prof Bunzo Tsuji
Kobe Univ, Faculty of Engr
Rokkodai-cho, Nada-ku
Kobe   657

Mr Katsuyoshi Tsukamoto
Tokyo Gas Co Ltd
1-16-25 Shibaura
Minato-ku, Tokyo   105

Sawada Tsutomu
Tokushima Univ
2-1 Minami-Josanjma
Tokushima   770

Dr Kazunori Uchida
Dept. Ag. Eng., Kyoto Univ.
Kitashirakawa, Sakyo-ku
Kyoto   606

Mr Kaoru Ueno
Kajima Inst. of Const. Tech.
19-1,2-chome, Tobitakyu
Chofu, Tokyo   182

Dr Yasufumi Umehara
Port and Harbour Research Inst.
1-1-3-chome Nagase
Yokosuka

Mr Takeshi Utsunomiya
Shikoku Electric Power Co Inc
2-5 Marunouchi,Takamatsu
Kagawa, Tokyo   760

Prof Minoru Wakabayashi
Dpri Kyoto University
Gokasho
Uji, Kyoto   611

Prof Hiroyuki Watanabe
Saitama University
Shimo Ohkubo 255
Urawa-Shi, Saitama   338

Dr Katsuyoshi Yamabe
Japan Univ. Prod. Engr.
1-2-1 Izumi-cho
Narashino, Chiba   275

Mr Makoto Yamagata
Chiyoda Chemical Eng. & Const.
12-1 Tsurumichuo 2-Chome Tsurumi-Ku
Yokohama   230

Mr Tetsuro Yamamoto
Tech J.C. Univ of Yamaguchi
Tokiwadai 2557
Ube-shi, Yamaguchi   755

Mr Koji Yanabu
Osaka Gas Co Ltd
Higashi-ku Hirano-machi 5-1
Osaka   541

Dr Shintaro Yao
Kansai University
Yamate-cho 3
Suita, Osaka   564

Prof Kuniaki Udagawa
Tokyo Denki Univ
2-2 Nishiki-Cho
Kanda, Chiyoda-ku, Tokyo   101

Mr Sumio Umebayashi
Chiyoda Chimical Eng. & Const.
12-1 Tsurumichuo 2-chome Tsurumi-ku
Yokohama   230

Prof Hajime Umemura
Shibaura Inst of Tech
3-9-14 Shibaura
Minato-ku,Tokyo   108

Prof Akira Wada
Dept. of Arch - Tokyo Inst. of Tech.
2-12-1 Ookayama
Meguro-ku, Tokyo   152

Mr Fumio Watanabe
Kyoto Univ.
Yoshida Honmachi, Sakyoku
Kyoto   606

Mr Minoru Watanabe
Urban Economic Inst
Shinbashi 5-8-13
Minato-ku, Tokyo   105

Prof Yoshikazu Yamada
Kyoto Univ.
Dpt Cvl Eng Kyoto U. Sakyo-ku
Kyoto   606

Dr Shizuo Yamamoto
Chiyoda Chemical Eng. & Const.
3-1-4 Ikegami Shin Cho
Kawasaki, Kanagawa   210

Dr Hiroyuki Yamanouchi
Building Research Inst.
1 Tatehara Oho-Macni
Tsukuba, Japan   305

Prof Eiji Yanagsawa
Tohoku Univ.
Dept. of Civil Eng. Faculty of Eng
Sendai   980

Harumi Yashiro
Waseda Univ
54-83 Shiboguchi Takatu-ku
Kawasaki, Kanagawa

Mr Kazuhiro Yoshida
Ohsaki Research Institute
Fuk. Sei. Bld 2-2-2 Uch-cho, Chi-ku
Tokyo   100

Mr Nozomu Yoshida
Sato Kogyo Co. Ltd.
47-3 Santa
Atsugi, Kanagawa   243-02

Prof Soji Yoshikawa
Kyoto University
Disaster Prev. Res. Institute
Gokanosho, Uji, Kyoto   611

Kido Yoshikazu
Kumagaigumi

Shinjyuku, Tokyo

Prof Yoshiaki Yoshimi
Tokyo Institute of Technology
2-12-1 O-okayama, Meguro-ku
Tokyo   152

Prof Koji Yoshimura
Oita Univ.
700 Dan-no-haru, Dept. Arch. Eng
Oita   870-11

Dr Shizuyo Yoshizawa
Earthquake Research Inst.
U of Tokyo Yay. 1-1-1 Bunkyo-ku
Tokyo   113

Jordan

Mr. Amjad F Barghouthi
Univ. of Jordan
School of Engineering
Amman

Dr Musa R Resheidat
Yarmouk Univ
Dept Cvl Engr
Irbid

Kuwait

Dr. Husain Al-Khait
Kuwait Univ.
P.O. Box 17421
Khaldiah

Dr. Hasan Askar
Kuwait Univ.
College of Eng., Dept of Civil Eng
Khaldia

Malaysia

Mr Leyuchong Hua
SEASEE
c®o Malaysian Mtr Ser Jalan Sultan
Petaling Jaya

Mr Shu Y Khoon
Geological Srvy Of Malaysia

Mexico

Mr Jaime M Antoniano
A.G.M.
Bosque De Duraznos #65-708-b
Mexico City   11700

G. R Aranda-h
Instituto De Ingenierea, UNAM
Apdo. 70-472
Coyoacair

Prof Gustavo A Ayala
Instituto de Ingenieria
Ciudad Univ APDO-70-642
Mexico City   04510

Prof Enrique Del Valle
National U. of Mexico
Div de Est de P.G. Fac de Ing, UNAM
Cd. Universitaria, Mexico D.F. 04510

Prof Luis Esteva
Ins Engr Univ of Mexico

Mexico City

Mr Ramiro G Gonzalez-Davila
A.G.M.
Av. Nuevo Leon #209-601
Mexico City   06170

Dr Oscar Hernandez Basilio
Instituto de Investigaciones Electri
Apart. 70-561 Ciudad Univ
Mexico City   CP 04510

Vazquez Z Macario
Petroleos Mexicanos
14 De Agosto 33
Mexico City, Mexico   11610

Moreno A Miguel
Ins Mexicano del P
Av de los cien metros #152
Mexico City   2P14

Bonifacio Pena-Pardo
U. Veracruzana
Costa Verde #301
Veracruz

Prof Octavio A Rascon
National Autonomous Univ. of Mexico
Ciudad Univ. - Facultad De Ing.
Mexico City, Distrito Federal 06000

Oscar G Reynoso
U. Auto Metro-Xoch Div CYAD
Calzada Hueso Esq Canal Nac Coapa
Mexico City

Prof Francisco J Sanchez-Sesma
Instituto de Ingenieria, UNAM
Cd. Universitaria, Apdo 70-472
Mexico City   04510

Dr Mario Chavez
Instituto De Ingenieria, Unam
Apdo. 70-569
Mexico City   04510

Mr Agustin Escobar
Antisismicos SSS
Uruapan #3 5 Piso Col Roma
Mexico City   06700

Mr Andres E Fernandez
Mapire Re
H. De Padeirna 107-6
Mexico City   10200

Mr Raul Grandados
P.E.S.A.
Silos 110
Mexico City   09810

Octavio B Luna
Mexican Petroleum Inst
Av 100 Metros #152
Mexico City

Roberto Meli
Nat Univ Of Mexico
Ciudad Univ
Mexico City

Luis Munguia
Cicese
Espinosa #843
Ensenada, Baja Calif

Prof Jorge Prince
Inst. of Engr. Univ. of Mexico
Cd. Universitaria
Mexico City   04510

Mr Alfonso Reyes
CICESE
Espinoza 843
Ensenada, Baja California   22830

Prof Emilio Rosenblueth
Universidad Nacional Autonoma De Mex
Instituto De Ingenieria
Ciudad Universitaria

Yanez Soto
Pemex Smis
Cuavhtenioc 54 San Pablo Ted.
Mexico City   21

Prof Jeseluis Trigos
Buffte Industrial
Apartado 74-171
Mexico City   09080

Mr Mauricio N Voorduin
Muenchener de Mexico
Jose Ma Velasco 30 Col San Jose Ins
Mexico City   03900

Mr Adolfo E Zeevaert
Consulting
Torre LatAm. 2506 Lazaro Cardenas#2
Mexico City   06007

Morocco

Dr Khalid Ramdane
Nat'l Mohamedia Sch of Engr

Rabat

Netherlands

Mr Joop Den Uije
Delft Univ of Tech
Stevinweg 1
Delft   2628 CN

New Zealand

Mr Henry Bayly
Wellington Regional Council
203-209 Willis St.
Wellington

Dr. Ian Brown
DSIR
P O Bx 30368
Lower Hutt

Mr George C Clifton
New Zealand Hvy Eng Rsrch Assoc
PO Bx 76-134
Auckland

Dr Barry J Davidson
Univ Auckland
Private Bag
Auckland

Mr Ross W Fischer
Chf. Civ. Eng. Off., N.Z. Rail
Private Bag
Wellington

Dr David L Hutchison
Ministry of Work & Developement
PO Bx 12041
Wellington North

Dr Murray L Jacobs
Consulting Engineer
21 Ridings Rd Remuera
Auckland

Mr Terence J Kayes
Tonkin & Taylor Ltd
PO Bx 12-152
Wellington

Mr John M Leuchars
Smith Leuchars Ltd
Ste 200 T&G Bld Wellesley St
Auckland

Mr D S Mackenzie
Mackenzie & Green
72 Grafton Rd
Auckland

Dr John B Mander
New Zealand Railways
22 Chittick Place
Wanganui

Mr Warwick D McWha
Repco Engr
P.O. Bx 22-177
Otahuhu

Mr Bryce M Morris
Insurance Consultant
24 Norwich Street
Wellington,, New Zealand   6001

Dr Arthur J O'Leary
Morrison, Cooper & Partners
P. O. Box 6214
Wellington

Prof Thomas Paulay
University of Canterbury
Dept. of Civil Engineering
Christchurch

Dr Robert I Skinner
Physics & Engr Lab
Private Bag Lower Hutt
Wellington

Mr Brian J Wood
Consulting Engr
PO Bx 701
Christchurch

Dr Bernard M McNamee

39A Creyke Road Flat 2
Christchurch 4

Mr Leslie M Megget
Victoria Univ.
Private Bag
Wellington

Mr Kenneth S Mulholland
Wellington City Council
7 Ashleigh Crescent
Wellington 3

Prof Robert Park
University of Canterbury
Private Bag
Christchurch

Dr Richard D Sharpe
Beca,Carter,Hollings,Ferner Ltd
P.O. Bx 3942
Wellington

Dr Warren R Walpole
Univ of Canterbury
Private Bag
Christchurch

Nicaragua

Dr Celina U Penalba
Universidad Centroamericana
Reparto Belmonte #21 Rm 6-1/2
Managua

Norway

Prof Hilmar Bungum
NTNF/NORSAR
POBx 51
Kjeller   N-2007

Dr Harold B Hansteen
Norwegian Geot. Institute
NGI, P. O. Box 40 Taasen
Oslo 8   0801

Dr Jostein Hellesland
Dr Ing A Aas-Jakobsen A/S
Parkveien 57
Oslo 2

Steinar Hetland
Norwegian Cont
Hausmannsgate 34 PO Bx 40
Andertorget, Oslo

Mr Marc Lefranc
Aker Ingineering
Tjuoholmen
Oslo 2

Mr Christian Madshus
Norwegian Geotech Inst
NGI POBx 40 Taasen
Olso 8   0801

Dr Farrokh Nadim
Norwegian Geotechnical Institute
Ngi, P.O. Box 40 Taasen
Oslo 8   0801

Mr Oddvar Slettevold
Aker Engineering A/S
Tjuvholmen
Oslo 2

Peru

Mr Juan Bariola
Pont U Catolica Peru Dpt Ing

Lima 21

Dr Marcial Blondet
Catholic U. of Peru
Dpt de Ing Apart 12534
Lima 21   21

Mr Jose L Bosio
Jose Luis Bosio V. Ingenieros Consul
Av Prim 120 Of B503 Sant de Surco
Lima   33

Maria Jesus H De Vargas

Benavides 1480 7B
Lima

Mr Gonzalez V Dimas
Procasa
San Jose #332
Arequipa

Prof Julio Kuroiwa
National University of Engineering
Av. del Parque Sur 442, Corpac
Lima   27

Mr Julio V Neumann
Univ Catolica Peru

Lima 21

Mr Raul Rios
G.R.C.U.I.A.I.C.
Av Central 671 Of 801
Lima   27

Mr Daniel Torrealva
Lab de Est Pont Univ Catolica Peru
Apartado Postal 12534
Lima 21

Philippines

Mr. Romeo S Caparros
A.S.E.P.
65 E. Abada, Loyola Hgts.
Quezon, Metro Manila

Mrs Lolita Garcia

Pagasa

Dr Andres O Hizon
N.S.S.E.E.P.
160-A Panay Av co E delos Santos Av
Quezon

Dr Angel L Lazaro, III
N.S.S.E.E.P.
160-A Panay Av core delos Santos Av
Quezon City

Mr Rolando G Valenzuela
Seasee
c®o Pagasa 1424 Quezon Ave
Quezon City

Portugal

Mr Eduardo C Carvalmo
Nat Lab for Civil Enge
Av Brasil 101
Lisbon   1799

Prof Ricardo T Duarte
Lab Nat De Engenharia Civil
101 Av Do Brasil
Lisbon   1799

Luiz A Mendes-Victor
Inst Mat Met Geo
Rua C Do Aeroporto
Lisbon

Mr Carlos S Oliveira
Nat Lab of Cvl Engr
Av Brasil 101
Lisbon

Dr Luis C Simoes
Univ of Coimbra-Portugal
Qta. S. Miguel-Solum
Coimbra   3000

Puerto Rico

Mr Milton R Martinez
Watson & Villate
5 Acacia St Monterry Ind Park
San Juan   00920

Dr Milto R Martinez-Delgado
College of Engineering
Univ of Puerto Rico Mayaguez Campus
Mayaguez   00708

Prof Luis R Perez
Univ. of Puerto Rico
College of Eng./Gen. Eng. Dept.
Mayaguez   00708

Dr Leandro Rodriguez-Agrait
College of Engineering
Univ of Puerto Rico Mayaguez Campus
Mayaguez   00708

Dr Miguel Santiago-Melendez
College of Engineering
Univ of Puerto Rico Mayaguez Campus
Mayaguez   00708

Romania

Mr. Alexandru Cismigiu
Architectural Institute
N: 18-20 Academiei, Sectors
Bucharest

Saudi Arabia

Dr Syed A Ali
King Abdulaziz Univ, Jeddah
P.O.Box 9027, Civ. Eng.Dept Kaau
Jeddah

Singapore

Dr Thambirajah Balendra
National Univ. of Singapore
Kent Ridge Campus
                    0511

South Africa

Dr Daniel J Wium
Van Wyk and Louw Inc
PO Bx 905
Pretoria   0001

Spain

Dr. Alberto Bernal
Spanish Seismic Assoc.

Madrid

Alfonso Lopez-Arroyo
Ins Geo Nat
Ibanez Ibero 3
Madrid   28028

Prof Jose L Justo
Univ of Seville
E.T.S. Arqu-Avda Reina Mercedes Sin
Sevilla

Mr Claudio Olalla
Ministerio Obras Publicas
Alfonso XII #3
Madrid 7

Sweden

Mr. Anders Bodare
VBB Consultants/Royal Inst Tech
Spetsuagen 6
Uppsala, Stockholm   S-7S2 57

Mr Birger R Nilsson
ASEA AB
Dept KYBA
Vasteras   S-721 83

Switzerland

Dr Ernst Berger
Basler & Hofmann
Forchstrasse 395
Zurich   8029

Mr Hans Furrer
Motor-Columbus Consulting Engr. Inc.
Parkstrasse 27
Baden   CH-5401

Dr Haydar E Ermutlu
EMCH & Berger Bern AG
Gartenstrasse 1
Bern   CH- 3001

Mr Daniel G Kluge
HSK
HSK
Wuerinlingen   5303

Switzerland (cont)

Dr Bruno O Porro
Swiss Re
50/60 Mythenquai
Zurich   CH-8022

Mr Dario Somaini
Swis Federal Institute of Technology
ETH-Honggerberg
Zurich   CH-8093

Dr Konrad Staudacher
Swiss Federal Institute of Technolog
Frohburestr. 85
Zurich   CH-8006

Mr Dieter Wepf
Swiss Federal Institute of Technolog
1BK, Eth-Hoenggerberg
Zurich   CH-8093

Dr John P Wolf
Electowatt Engr Services Ltd
P.O. Bx 8022
Zurich

Thailand

Dr Prinya Nutalya
Asian Inst of Tech

Dr Martin Wieland
Asian Inst of Tech
AIT Box 2754
Bangkok   10501

Dr Yasuo Yamada
Asian Inst of Tech
GPO Box 2754
Bangkok   10501

The Netherlands

Mr. John M Spijkers
Delft Univ. of Technology
1 Stevinweg
Delft   2628 CN

Turkey

Attila Askar
Bogazici Univ

Bebek, Istanbul

Dr Mustafa O Erdik
Middle East Tech Univ
Equake Eng Rsrch Cntr M.E. Tech U.
Ankara

Prof Ugur Ersoy
Middle East Technical Univ.
Dept. of Civil Eng.
Ankara

Prof Polat Gulkan
Hacetepe Univ
Fac of Engr Hacettepe Univ
Ankara

Ahmet Tabban
Min Of Pblc Wrks Resetlement
Gen Direct of Bldg Mat EQ Rsrch
Ankara

Prof Rifat Yarar
Tech Univ of Istanbul
Taksim-Taskisla
Istanbul

Prof Ahmed M Abdel-Ghaffar
Princeton Univ
Civil Engineering Dept.
Princeton, NJ   08544

Haldar Achintya
GA Inst of Tech
Sch of Cvl Engr
Atlanta, GA   30084

Mr Samy A Adham
Agbabian Assoc.
250 N. Nash
El Segundo, CA   90245

Mr Rashid Ahmad
Calif. Dept. of Water Resources
921 11th St Bx 388
Sacramento, CA   95802

Prof Keiiti Aki
MIT
54-526,MIT
Cambridge, MA   02139

Mr. Haluk M Aktan
Wayne State Univ
667 Merrick
Detroit, MI   48202

Mr Ali Al-Ghothani

651 Cuyahoga St.
Columbus, OH   43210

Dr S. T Algermissen
USGS
Den. Fed. Center Box 25046 MS966
Denver, CO   80224

Mr. Matthew G Allen
Corps of Engineers
650 Capitol Mall
Sacramento, CA   95814

Dr Amin M Almuti
Bechtel National Inc.
45 Fremont 16C4, P.O. Box 3965
San Francisco, CA   94119

Dr Jose I Alvarez-Baleriola
Instituto Eduardo Torroja
816 Norvell St
El Cerrito, CA   94530

Prof Daniel P Abrams
Univ. of Colorado
Univ. Colorado Civil Eng. Box 428
Boulder, CO   80309

Mr. Barry L Adelson
Exxon Production Research Co.
P.O. Box 2189
Houston, TX   77001

Dr Mihran S Agbabian
Agbabian Associates
250 N. Nash St.
El Segundo, CA   90245

Prof Goodarz Ahmadi
Clarkson Univ
MIE Clarkson Univ
Potsdam, NY   13676

Dr. A. E Aktan
LSU
Assoc. Prof. of Civil Eng.
Baton Rouge, LA   70803

Mr. Ibtisam Al Masri
George Washington Univ.
511 Four Mile Road #502
Alexandria, VA   22305

Mr Gifford H Albright
National Science Foundation
1800 G Street, Nw. Room 1130
Washington, D.C.   20550

Mr Edmund W Allen
E.W. Allen & Associates
16 Exchange Place
Salt Lake City, UT   84111

Dr. Robert H Allen
Dept. of Mechanical Engineering
Univ. of Houston
Houston, TX   77004

Mr Leonardo Alvarez

1648 Danromas Way
San Jose, CA   95129

Mr Mohamed N Alyagshi Eilouch
Ohio State Univ.
613 Stark Ct.
Columbus, OH   43210

Mr Abdelmoniem M Amin

589 Stinchcomb Dr., #3
Columbus, OH 43202

Mr Ali Amini
Kinemetrics, Inc.
222 Vista Avenue
Pasadena, CA 91107

Mr William C Andberg
Fed Energy Regulatory Comm.
333 Market St 6th Fl.
San Francisco, CA 94105

Dr John G Anderson
Univ. of CA San Diego
IGPP (A-025)
La Jolla, CA 92093

Dr Thomas L Anderson
Fluor Engineers, Inc.
3333 Michelson Dr.
Irvine, CA 92730

Mr. Rodrigo Araya
Univ. of Chile
834 Riley Dr. #84
Albany, CA 94706

Dr Ralph Archuleta
USGS
345 Middlefield Road
Menlo Park, CA 94025

Mr. Christopher Arnold
Building Systems Development
3130 Le Selic - Suite 308
San Mateo, CA 94403

Prof Hassan Astaneh
Univ. of Oklahoma
202 W. Boyd, Room 334
Norman, OK 73091

Dr Richard H Atkinson
Atkinson-Noland & Assoc.
2619 Spruce St
Boulder, CO 80302

Mr. Gilbert A Avila
Corps of Engineers
650 Capitol Mall
Sacramento, CA 95814

Mr. Navin R Amin
Skidmore, Owings & Merrill
130 Sutter St.
San Francisco, CA 94104

Ms Thalia Anagnos
Stanford Univ
Dept. of Civil Eng. Stanford Univ.
Stanford, CA 94305

Prof James C Anderson
U. of Southern California
30219 Via Rivera
Rancho Palos Verdes, CA 90274

Mr Robert D Anderson
ABKJ Inc Engr
1300 Dexter Horton Bld
Seattle, WA 98104

Prof A. H Ang
Univ. of Illinois
208 N. Romine
Urbana, IL 61801

Prof John C Archea
Georgia Ins of Tech
College of Arch
Atlanta, GA 30332

Dr Teoman Ariman
Univ. of Tulsa
Col. of Engr & Applied Sci.
Tulsa, OK 74104-3189

Dr. Alejandro Asfura
Impell Corp.
350 Lennon Lane
Walnut Creek, CA 94598

Dr Selcuk T Atalik
Bechtel Power Corp
12400 E. Imperial Highway
Norwalk, CA 90650

Mr Mark A Austin

2442 Peidmont Ave #19
Berkeley, CA 94704

Joao J Azevedo
Stanford University
John A. Blume EE Center
Stanford, CA 94305

Dr Kenji Baba
Univ. of Illinois
3113 NCEL Univ of IL, 208 N. Romine
Urbana, IL   61801

Dr Thomas J Baca
Sandia National Laboratories
P.O. Box 5800
Albuquerque, NM   87185

Mr Brent P Ballif
L. H. Ballif Associates
477 Taft, P. O. Box 4052
Pocatello, ID   83201

Dr Prabodh B Banavalkar
CBM Engineers, Inc.
1700 West Loop South, Suite 830
Houston, TX   77027

Mr Shyama Banerjee
United Nations
F-ship Srv 2 UN Plaza Rm DC2-0424
New York, NY   10017

Mr. Jean-Pierre Bardet
Univ. of Southern California
Civil Eng Dept, VHE 406 Univ Park
Los Angeles, CA   90089-0242

Mr. Richard M Barker
Virginia Tech
C E Dept , 200 Patton
Blacksburg, VA   24061

Mr Robert E Barsam
Los Angeles County Road Dept.
1540 Alcazar St.
Los Angeles, CA   90033

Mr Mac T Bautista
Fed Energy Reg Comm
333 Market St 6th Fl.
San Francisco, CA   94105

Prof Donald E Baxa
Univ of Wisconsin-Extension
432 N Lake St Rm 735
Madison, WI   53706

R.G. Bea
PMB Systems Engr
500 Sansome St Ste 400
San Francisco, CA   94111

Dr James E Beavers
Martin Marietta Energy Systems Inc
PO Bx Y Bld 9733-4 MS 2
Oak Ridge, TN   37831

Prof James L Beck
Cal Tech
Mail Code 104-44
Pasadena, CA   91125

Ms Ann M Becker
Dames & Moore
4321 Directors Row
Houston, TX   77092

Prof Carlos G Bell

UNCC Station
Charlotte, NC   28223

Ms Bernice K Bender
USGS
Ms 966 Denver Federal Center
Denver, CO   80225

Dr Fouad M Bendimerad
Stanford University
48A Escondido Village
Stanford, CA   94305

Mr Lee Benuska
Kinemetrics
222 Vista Avenue
Pasadena, CA   91107

Mr Leon L Beratan
U.S. Nuclear Reg. Comm.
Mail Stop SS-1130
Washington, D.C.   20555

Prof Glen V Berg
Univ of Michigan
1033 Baldwin Ave
Ann Arbor, MI   48104

Mr Hal Bernson
City of Los Angeles Council
200 N Spring St #236
Los Angeles, CA   91436

Mr Dennis L Berry
Andersen Bjornstad Kane Jacobs
500 L Street, Suite 401
Anchorage, AK   99501

Mr Vitelmo V Bertero
Univ. of California
783 Davis Hall, Univ. of Cal.
Berkeley, CA   94720

Prof Jacobo Bielak
Carnegie-Mellon Univ
Dept of Civil Engr
Pittsburgh, PA   15213

Philip Birkeland
ABAM Engrs Inc
500 S. 336th St
Washington, D.C.   98003

Mr. Alex Bittenbinder
Newt Inc.
3206 16th Ave. W. Suite B
Seattle, WA   98119

Mr William H Blair
Alameda Co. Water District
380 So. Fremont Blvd. P.O. Box 5110
Fremont, CA   94537

Mr Thomas F Bohannan
Facilities Management/Pacific Medica
Clay at Buchanan
San Francisco, CA   94120

Prof Bruce A Bolt
Univ of California, Berkely
1491 Greenwood Terrace
Berkeley, CA   94708

Ms Carolyn S Boord
URS/John A. Blume Engrs.
130 Jessie Street
San Francisco, CA   94105

Mr. Suresh Boral
Advance Engineers Ltd.
6207 Od Keene 211 Ct.
Springfield, VA   22152

Dr Sidney F Borg
Stevens Inst. Of Tech

Hoboken, NJ   07030

Mr Bill H Bowerman
LTV Energy Products Co
PO BX 670
Arlington, TX   76010

Mr Richard V Bettinger
PG&E
77 Beale St. Rm. 2653
San Francisco, CA   94106

Mr. John I Bilco
S.C.R.T.D.
425 S. Main St
Los Angeles, CA   90013

Mr Arvind K Bisarya
H.B.E. Corp
11330 Olive Blvd POBx 27339
St. Louis, MO   63141

Ms Martha L Blair
William Spangle & Assco. Inc.
3240 Alpine Road
Portola Valley, CA   94025

Mr Robert Blukis
Fed Energy Reg Com
333 Market St 6th Fl
San Francisco, CA   94105

Dr Auguste C Boissonnade

113 A Escondido Village
Stanford, CA   94305

Dr Patricia A Bolton
Battelle Seattle Research Center
4000 NE 41st Street
Seattle, WA   98105

Dr David M Boore
USGS
345 Middlefield Road
Menlo Park, CA   94025

Dr Roger D Borcherdt
USGS
345 Middlefield Road
Menlo Park, CA   94025

Mr Robert D Bourn
Bonn. Power Adm
2355 SE 7th Ave
West Linn, OR   97068

Dr A. G Brady
USGS
345 Middlefield Road
Menlo Park, CA   94025

Mr Frank W Brady
PG&E
77 Beale St. Rm. 2619
San Francisco, CA   94106

Dr Gregg E Brandow
Brandow & Johnston Assoc.
1660 West Third St.
Los Angeles, CA   90017

Mr David C Breiholz
David C Breiholz & Co, Inc
1852 Lomita Blvd
Lomita, CA   90717

Mr George W Brodt
Los Angeles Dept. of Water and Power
111 N. Hope Street, Rm 1032
Los Angeles, CA   91344

Dr Dan Brown
Andrew Structures
P.O. Box 1039
Kansas City, MO   64152

Mr John E Brown
Brown & Lindsey
2722 Hyde St.
San Francisco, CA   94109

Mr Michael L Brown
Helix Water District
8111 Univ Ave
La Mesa, CA   92041

Mr Robert A Bruce
H.J. Degenkolb Assoc.
350 Sansome St, Ste 500
San Francisco, CA   94104

Norm Brudigain
TEI Engr
PO Bx 24075
Oakland, CA   94608

Prof James N Brune
Univ. of Calif., San Diego
IGPP (A-025)
La Jolla, CA   92093

Mr John C Burton
Rutherford & Chekene
487 Bryant Street
San Francisco, CA   94107

Mr Vincent R Bush
Int Conf of Bldg Ofcls
5360 S Workman Mill Rd
Whittier, CA   90601

Mr Theodore E Bushnell
Portland General Electric
121 SW Salmon St
Portland, OR   97204

William S Butcher
National Science Foundation
1800 G. Street, N.W.
Washington, D.C.   20550

Dr David L Butler
MicroGeophysics Corp
10900 W 44th Av
Wheat Ridge, CO   80033

Martin Button
Comptech Engr Srv
2855 Telegraph Ave Ste 410
Berkeley, CA   94705

Prof Ahmet S Cakmak
Princeton University
Dept. Of Civil Engineering
Princeton, NJ   08544

Dr Kenneth W Campbell
USGS
Den. Fed. Center, MS966
Denver, CO   80225

Mr Ted J Canon
H.J. Degenkolb Assoc.
350 Sansome St.
San Francisco, CA   94104

Mr Michael P Caracostas
Moti Trading Co
666 E. Ocean Blv Apt 2408
Long Beach, CA   90802

Mr. Billy L Carnahan
L.T.V. Energy Products Co.
P.O. Bx 670
Arlington, TX   76010

Mr. L. Carpenter
Skidmore, Owings, & Merrill
70 Universal City Plaza
Universal City, CA   91608

Dr James R Carr
Univ. Of Missouri-Rolla
Dept. Of Geological Eng. - Umr
Rolla, MO   65401

Mr. Mehmet Celebi
USGS/SFSU
502 Nottingham Lane
Foster City, CA   94404

Mr. Andrew C Chang
Northrop Corp.
1 Northrop Ave
Hawthorne, CA   90250

Mr I-Kwang Chang
Stanford Univ John Blume EEC
Civil Engr Dept
Stanford, CA   94305

Dr Ming-Du Chang
Kaiser Engr Hanford Co
PO Bx 888
Richland, WA   99352

Mr Donald Chappell
Forell/Elsesser Engineers, Inc.
539 Bryant Street
San Francisco, CA   94107

Dr. Chunduri V Chelapati
Cal State Univ Long Beach
1250 Bellflower Bl Dept Cvl Eng
Long Beach, CA   90840

Dr J.C. Chen
UC Lawrence Livermore Lab
P. O. Box 808, L-95
Livermore, CA   94550

Mr Yong-ming Chen
Fed Energy Reg Comm
333 Market St 6th Fl.
San Francisco, CA   94105

Prof Franklin Y Cheng
Univ of Missouri-Rolla
1307 Highland Dr
Rolla, MO   65401

Mr Wei-Ling Chiang
John A. Blume Center
P. O. Box 2987
Stanford, CA   94305

Mr Mark S Caspe
M.S. Caspe Co.
1640 Oakwood Dr.
San Mateo, CA   94403

Prof Jean-Lou A Chameau
Purdue Univ.
Dept of Civil Eng., Purdue Univ.
West Lafayette, IN   47907

Mr. Frank K Chang
Waterways Experiment Station
P.O. Box 631
Vicksburg, MS   39180

Mr Jeng I Chang
U.S. Army So. Pac. Div.
630 Sansome St., Room 1233
San Francisco, CA   94111

Dr Nien-Yin Chang
Dept Civil Engineering U. Colorado
1100 14th St.
Denver, CO   80202

Mr. Manmohan S Chawla
G.S.A.
19th & F Sts. N.W., Room 3310
Washington, D.C.   20405

C. K Chen
URS/John A. Blume & Assoc. Eng.
130 Jessie St.
San Francesco, CA   94105

Dr. P.C. Chen
Interpacific Tech Inc
180 Grand Ave, Suite 900
Oakland, CA   94612

Prof James A Cheney
Univ. of Calif. Davis
Dept. of Civil Engineering
Davis, CA   95616

Dr Thomas M Cheng
US Nuclear Regulatory Commission
10102 Alsace Court
Great Falls, VA   22066

Mr Robert Chieruzzi
LeRoy Crandall and Assoc.
711 North Alvarado Street
Los Angeles, CA   90026

180

Mr. Nilesh C Chokshi
U.S. Nuclear Reg. Comm.
MS P 214
Washington, D.C.   20555

Prof Anil K Chopra
University of California
Dept of Civil Engineering
Berkeley, CA   94720

Dr Andrew K Chou
PG&E
77 Beale St. Rm. 2648
San Francisco, CA   94106

Mr. Foo L Chow
The 4th Dist. Res. Inst.
240 Hyde St.
San Francisco, CA   94102

Ted Christensen
Wheeler & Gray
7462 N. Figueroa
Los Angeles, CA   91206

Dr John T Christian
Stone & Webster Eng. Corp.
245 Summer St. - Box 2325
Boston, MA   02107

JR Christiansen
IBM
5600 Cottle Rd
San Jose, CA   95193

Mr. Dae H Chung
Lawrence Livermore Nat. Lab.
P.O. Box 808, Code L-95
Livermore, CA   94550

Mr. Riley M Chung
Nat'l Bureau of Stds
Building 226, Room B162
Goithersburg, MD   20799

Mr. Kuo Chung-Ming
Northrop Aircraft
1 Northrop Ave
Hawthorne, CA   90250

Mr Allen J Clark
MTS Systems Corp
Box 24012
Minniapolis, MN   55424

Cpt David L Clawson
Corps of Engrs
211 Main St
San Francisco, CA   94105

Dr Douglas P Clough
ABAM Engr Inc
500 S 336th St
Federal Way, WA   98003

Prof Ray W Clough
Univ. of California
576 Vistamont Ave.
Berkeley, CA   94708

Mr Lloyd S Cluff
Woodward-Clyde
33 Mt Spring Ave
San Francisco, CA   94114

Mr John D Coates
Factory Mutual Eng. Assoc.
1000 4 St. Suite 700, P.O. Box 7020
San Rafael, CA   94901

Dr David W Coats
Lawrence Livermore Lab
P. O. Box 808
Livermore, CA   94550

Dr Douglas A Coats
Exxon Production Research
P. O. Box 2189
Houston, TX   77001

Mr David A Cole
Dowl Engineers
4040 "B" St.
Anchorage, AK   99503

Mr Eugene E Cole
Cole, Yee, Schubert & Associates
1515 River Park Drive, Suite 220
Sacramento, CA   95815-4684

Mr Frank Conati
MTS Systems Corp
Box 24012
Minniapolis, MN   55424

Mr Milton E Contreras
Rice Univ.
Dept. of Civil Engineering-Box 1892
Houston, TX   77251

Mr. James D Cooper
D.N.A.
6810 Telegraph Road
Alexandtia, VA   22310

Mr Thomas W Cooper
T. W. Cooper, Inc.
Box 4253
Torrance, CA   90510

Dr W. G Corley
Portland Cement Assoc.
5240 Old Orchard Road
Skokie, IL   60077

Dr. Allin Cornell
Stanford Univ
110 Coquito Way
Portola Valley, CA   94025

Prof Carl J Costano
City Univ. of New York
Dept of Civil Eng. , Convent Ave
New York, NY   10031

Dr James F Costello
U.S.N.R.C.
Mail Stop 5650 NL
Washington, D.C.   20555

Mr. John W Cox
Tera, Inc
P.O. Box 740038
Houston, TX   77274

Prof James I Craig
Georgia Institute of Technology
Aerospace Engineering
Atlanta, GA   30332

Mr L.L. Crandall
LeRoy Crandall and Associates
711 North Alvarado Street
Los Angeles, CA   90026-4099

Mr Donald J Croft
Tudor Engineering Co.
149 New Montgomery St.
San Francisco, CA   94105

Ms Betty Croly
Alameda City Planning Dept
399 Elmhurst St #136
Hayward, CA   94544

Mr Daniel J Cross
MTS Systems Corp
Box 24012
Minneapolis, MN   55424

Dr C. B Crouse
Earth Technology
3777 Long Beach Blvd.
Long Beach, CA   90807

Mr Ernesto Cruz
U.C. Berkeley
195 Wilson St. # 73
Berkeley, CA   94710

Mr James H Cullen
Woodward-Clyde Consultants
100 Pringle Avenue
Walnut Creek, CA   94596

Mr Frederick C Cuny
Intertect
P. O. Box 10502
Dallas, TX   75207

Mr Edward A Danehy
Alameda Cnty Pblc Works Agency
399 Elmhurst St
Hayward, CA   94544

Mr Robert D Darragh
Dames & Moore
500 Sansome St
San Francisco, CA   94111

Mr Arthur C Darrow
Dames & Moore
812 Anacapa St Suite A
Santa Barbara, CA   93101

Dr Shamita Das
Lamont/Columbia Univ.

Palisades, NY   10964

Mr Richard F Davidson
U.S. Army Corps of Engrs.
HQ USACE (DAEN-ECE-G)
Washington, D.C.   20314

Dr John N Davies
Alaska Geol. Survey
c/o Geol. Inst. 903 Koyukuk Ave. N.
Fairbanks, AK   99701

Dr James F Davis
Cal Div of Mines & Geology
1416 Ninth St, Rm 1341
Sacramento, CA   95814

Mr Johan B DeReymaeker
De Heef America Inc
122 N Mill St
St Louis, MI   48880

Mr Henry J Degenkolb
H. J. Degenkolb Associates
350 Sansome Street, Suite 500
San Francisco, CA   94104

Dr Arnaldo T Derecho
Wiss, Janney, Elster Assoc, Inc
330 Pfingsten Rd
Northbrook, IL   60062

Mr John G Diehl
Kinemetrics, Inc.
222 Vista Ave.
Pasadena, CA   91107

Dr Neville C Donovan
Dames & Moore
500 Sansome St
San Francisco, CA   94111

Mr Robert J Downey
Tenn Valley Authority
400 Summit Hill TVA 2190 IBM-K
Knoxville, TN   37902

Mr Tom S Durham
Tennessee Emergency Management Agenc
3041 Sedco Drive
Nashville, TN   37204-1502

Mr Donald G Eagling
U.C. Lawrence Berkeley Lab
1 Cyclotron Rd, Bld 90, Rm 4128
Berkeley, CA   94720

Dr A.J. Eggenberger
National Science Foundation
1800 G Street, Nw. Rm 1130
Washington, D.C.   20550

Dr Mohammad R Ehsani
Univ. of Arizona
Dept. of Civil Engr.
Tucson, AR   85721

Mr Luis A De Bejar
Cornell Univ.
47-I Hasbrouk Apts.
Ithaca, NY   14850

Mr Clifton E Deal
Soil Conserv Srv
511 NW Broadway
Portland, OR   97059

Armen Der Kiureghian
U.C.
725 Davis Hall
Berkeley, CA   94608

Mr Arthur C Devine
City of Los Angeles
200 N. Spring Street, Room 960
Los Angeles, CA   90012

Prof Ricardo Dobry
Rensselaear Polytech
Dpt Cvl Eng
Troy, NY   12180

Dr Bruce M Douglas
Univ of Nevada Reno
Civil Engr Dept
Reno, NV   89557

Mr Jeffrey W Dulka
Pblc Wrks Dpt Pac Mis Tst Cntr
Code Pacific Mssle Test Cntr
Point Mugu, CA   93042

Prof Ahmad J Durrani
Rice University
Civil Engr. Dept, P. O. Box 1892
Houston, TX   77251

Mr John W Eaton
MCI Telecommunications Corp.
1150 17th St NW (071/037)
Washington, D.C.   20036

Mr Ronald T Eguchi
Agbabian Assoc.
250 N. Nash St
El Segundo, CA   90245

Mr Richard K Eisneri
Seismic Safety Commission
B.A.E.S. Hotel Claremont Studio Lvl
Berkeley, CA   94705

Prof Fathy M El-Kamshoshy
Cogswell College
600 Stockton Street
San Francisco, CA   94703

L Eldorado
Skidmore Owings & Merrill
70 Universal City Plaza
Universal City, CA   91608

Mr Shalom Eliahu
Engeo, Inc.
2280 Diamond Boulevard, Suite 200
Concord, CA   94520

Mr Guner Eruren
Cromwell Truemper Levy Parker & Wood
One Spring Street
Little Rock, AR   72201

Mr Alvaro F Espinosa
USGS
Den. Fed. Center, MS966
Denver, CO   80225

Joseph J Fedock
U.S.G.S.
345 Middlefield Rd., MS-77
Menlo Park, CA   94025

Prof Filip C Filippou
Univ. Of California Berkeley
777 Davis Hall, Dept Of Civ. Eng.
Berkeley, CA   94720

Mr Clement J Finney
Roman Catholic Diocese of Oakland
2900 Lakeshore Ave
Oakland, CA   94610

Mr Richard W Fischer
Calif. Dept. of Water Resources
7787 La Fiesta Way
Sacramento, CA   95828

Dr Jon P Fletcher
USGS
345 Middlefield Road
Menlo Park, CA   94025

Mr Dean A Focke
Ohio Disaster Serv Agency
2825 West Granville Rd
Worthington, OH   43085

Mr John H Elberling
Todco
230 Fourth St.
San Francisco, CA   94103

Mr Mark W Eli
LLNL
P.O. Box 808,L-390
Livermore, CA   94955

Mr Eric Elsesser
Forell/Elsesser Engineers, Inc.
539 Bryant Street
San Francisco, CA   94107

Mr Luis E Escalante
Los Angeles Dept. of Water & Power
P.O.Box 111, Room 1032 G.O.B.
Los Angeles, CA   90051

Mr Chris Evangel
Office of Management and Budget
New Exec. Office Bld. , Room 9236
Washington, D.C.   20053

Mr John M Ferritto
Navy Civil Engr Lab
Code L53
Port Hueneme, CA   93043

Dr John R Filson
USGS
905 National Center
Reston, VA   22092

Mr Hans J Fischer
Fischer-Stein Assoc
PO Bx 3007
Carbondale, IL   62901

Mr Jerome T Fishpaw
CRJG Associates
1080 Obrien Dr.
Menlo Park, CA   94025

Mr. Paul J Flores
S.C.E.P.P.
6850 Van Nuys Blvd., Suite 110
Van Nuys, CA   91405-4660

Mr Ka-Lun Fok
U.C. Berkeley, Dept of Civil Eng.
2708 College Ave, Apt. 14
Berkeley, CA   94705

Mr James W Foley Jr.
City of San Jose
801 N. First St. Room 300
San Jose, CA   95110

Mr Frank C Fong
Dept. of Water Resources
St. of CA, 921 11th Street
Sacramento, CA   95814

John Foss
Bell Comm Rsrch

Morristown, NJ   07960

Prof Douglas A Foutch
Univ. of Illinois
3108 Newmark Lab 208 N. Romine
Urbana, IL   61801

Robert A Frank
Applied Rsrch Assoc Inc
4917 Professional St
Raleigh, NC   27609

Prof Joseph B Franzini
Stanford University
Dept. of Civil Engineering
Stanford, CA   94305

Mr Sigmund A Freeman
Wiss,Janney,Elstner,Assoc.
2200 Powell St, Suite 925
Emeryville, CA   94608

G. R Fuller
US Dept of HUD
Rm 9156 HUD Bld
Washington, D.C.   20411

Mrs Angela K Gardner
Redwood City Bldg Dept
1017 Middlefield Rd PO Bx 391
Redwood City, CA   94064-0391

James H Gates
CalTrans Structures
PO Bx 1499
Sacramento, CA   95807

Mr William E Gates
Dames & Moore
20268 Corenzana Dr.
Woodland Hills, CA   91364

Fred E Followill
UC/ LLNL
PO Bx 808
Livermore, CA   94550

Mr Nicholas F Forell
Forell/Elsesser Engineers, Inc.
539 Bryant St.
San Francisco, CA   94107

Mr Jerry A Foster
ISO Commercial Risk Services, Inc.
2 Sylvan Way
Parsippany, NJ   07054

Mr Charles J Fox
Fox Howlett Industries
744 Folger Ave.
Berkeley, CA   94701

Dr Arley G Franklin
U.S. Army Engineer
Waterways Experiment Station
Vicksburg, MS   39180

Mr Gary E Freeland
Lawrence Livermore Nat'l Laboratory
P.O. Box 5506,L-799
Livermore, CA   94550

Prof Catherine E French(Wolfgram)
Univ. of Minnesota
244 CME 500 Pillsbury Dr. SE
Minneapolis, MN   55455-0220

S.R. Galletta
Bechtel Inc
50 Beale St
San Francisco, CA   94119

Mr Robert C Garrett
Sandia National Laboratories
7011 East Ave.
Livermore, CA   94550

Dr Nathan C Gates
Gulf Oil E & P Co
PO Bx 36506
Houston, TX   77236

Mr Carl A Gentry
John Carollo Engr
450 N. Wiget Lane
Walnut Creek, CA   94598

Mr Michael E Gerdts
M & M Protection Cons
3 Embarcadero Cntr #1280
San Francisco, CA   94111

Prof Peter Gergely
Cornell Univ.
Hollister Hall
Ithaca, NY   14853

Dr Mohsen Ghafory-Ashtiany
Mostazafan Found. of Iran/Bechtel Po
17600 Sequoia Dr. Apt # 301
Gaithersburg, MD   20877

Prof Satyendra K Ghosh
Univ of Illinois at Chicago
Dp Cvl Engr Mch & Mtlrgy POBx 4348
Chicago, IL   60680

Prof Lawrence Glaum
Univ of Alaska, Fairbanks
133 Duckering Bldg-306 Tanana Dr
Fairbanks, AK   99701

Mr Dawrence S Glenn

P.O. Box 181
Exeter, CA   93221

Prof Subhash C Goel
Univ of Michigan
Dept of Cvl Engr
Ann Arbor, MI   48109

Ms Paula L Gori
USGS
905 National Center
Reston, VA   22092

Mr Jim E Greenburg
INTEL Corp
3200 Lakeside Dr SC6-621
Santa Clara, CA   95050

Dr Patrick M Griffin
International Engineering Co., Inc.
180 Howard Street
San Francisco, CA   94105

Mr Richard A Gross
Industrial Risk Insurers
85 Woodland St
Hartford, CT   06102

Prof James M Gere
Stanford University
Dept. of Civil Engineering
Stanford, CA   94305

Prof J. Ghaboussi
University of Illinois
3106 Nwmrk Cvl Eng Lab 208 N Romine
Urbana, IL   61801

Mr Vincent J Ghio
PG&E
45 Fremont St. 23rd Floor
San Francisco, CA   94106

H.H. Givin
IBM/USC
645 Highland Ave
San Martin, CA   95046

Dr Dennis R Gle
Bechtel Power Corp.
P. O. Box 1000
Ann Arbor, MI   48106

Mr David C Glick
Naval Facilities Engineering Command
3358 La Mesa Dr. #3
San Carlos, CA   94070

Prof Barry J Goodno
Georgia Institute Of Technology
School Of Civil Engineering
Atlanta, GA   30332

Mr W. P Grant
Shannon & Wilson
1105 N. 38 St.
Seattle, WA   98103

Mr Robert Greenlaw
Allendale Mutual Insurance Co.
1301 Atwood Ave.
Johnston, RI   02919

Mr Karl K Gross
Bechtel Power Corp.
P. O. Box 3965
San Francisco, CA   94119

Mr Oue T Gudmestad
Statoil, Norway
c/o MIT, Dept of Civil Eng. 1-276
Cambridge, MA   02139

Mr Robert C Guenzler
EG&G Idaho, Inc.
P.O. Box 1625
Idaho Falls, ID   83415

Rachel M Gulliver
MESA 2 Inc
10901 Key West Ave
Northridge, CA   91326

Ajaya K Gupta
N.C. St Univ
Dpt Cvl Engr
Raleigh, NC   27695-7908

Mr Daniel J Guzy
US Nuclear Reg Comm
Mail Stop NL-5650
Washington, D.C.   20555

Dr Tarik A Hadj-Hamou
Tulane University
Dept. Of Civil Engineering
New Orleans, LA   70118

Mr Asadour H Hadjian
Bechtel Power Corp
12400 E. Imperial Hwy
Norwalk, CA   90650

Dr William W Hakala
National Science Foundation
1800 G Street, Nw
Washington, D.C.   20550

Mr Finn T Halbo
Stanford Linear Accelerator Center
2575 Sand Hill Road
Menlo Park, CA   94025

Prof John F Hall
Cal Tech
522 Hermosa Street
South Pasadena, CA   91030

Prof William Hall
Univ. of Illinois
1245 Newmark Lab, 208 N. Romine St.
Urbana, IL   61801

Mr John Hallenbeck
Hallenbeck and Assoc
1485 Park Ave
Emeryville, CA   94608

Marjorie L Halverson
Kinemetrics
222 Vista Ave
Pasadena, CA   91107

Dr Frank R Hand
F.R. Hand Consultants Inc
5701 Horton Rd.
Jackson, MI   49201

Mr. Nagy F Hanna
Ohio State Univ.
90 E. 14 Ave #V
Columbus, OH   43201

Mr Norman W Hanson
Portland Cement Assoc
Old Orchard Rd
Skokie, IL   60077

Prof Robert D Hanson
Univ. of Michigan
Dept. of Civil Eng - 304 WE
Ann Arbor, MI   48109

Mr Stanley A Hanusiak
PG&E
45 Fremont St 23rd Floor
San Francisco, CA   94106

Prof Maurice R Harlan
The Citadel, Mil Col of SC
106 Ashborough Ave
Summerville, SC   29483

Prof Medhat A Haroun
Univ. of Calif. at Irvine
Civil Eng. Dept.
Irvine, CA   92717

Dr. James R Harris
J.R. Harris & Co
1390 Logan St, Suite 217
Denver, CO   80203

Dr Gunnar A Harstead
Harstead Engr Assoc
169 Kinderkamack Rd
Park Ridge, NJ   07656

Mr Michael W Hart
Geocon Inc.
9530 Dowdy Dr
San Diego, CA   92126

Ahmed Hashish

5200 Anthony Wayne #712
Detriot, MI   48202

Timothy K Hasselman
Assoc Inc
2618 Via Rivera
Palos Verdes Estates, CA   90274

Prof Neil M Hawkins
Univ of Washington
201 More Hall FX-10
Seattle, WA   98195

Dr Walter W Hays
USGS
905 National Center
Reston, VA   22092

Ms Susan G Heikkala
Center for Plan. & Design
Univ. of Washington Mail Stop AL15
Seattle, WA   98195

Mr Frederick H Herzog
DuPont Co
Louviers Bldg
Wilmington, DE   19898

Mr Donald H Hillebrandt
Don Hillebrandt Assoc.
604 Mission St., #901
San Francisco, CA   94105

Dr Said I Hilmy
Rand Hll Comp Graphics
Cornell University
Ithaca, NY   14850

Mr Carlton L Ho
Stanford University
Dept. of Civil Engr. Terman Engr.
Stanford, CA   94305

Mr Edward P Hollis

P.O. Box 209
Palo Alto, CA   94302

Mr William T Holmes
Rutherford & Chekene
487 Bryant Street
San Francisco, CA   94107

Mr Richard C Haskell
Tridis Engineers
2118 Huntington Dr.
San Marino, CA   91108

Mr Don Hawkes
Utah Power & Light Co
PO Bx 899 Rm 247
Salt Lake City, UT   84110

Mr Joe H Haws
Shell Development
P.O. Box 1380
Houston, TX   77001

Mohammad A Heidari
Univ of S. CA
414 S. Virgil #121
Los Angeles, CA   90020

Mr George L Henderson

3137 Alanhill Lane
San Mateo, CA   94403

Mr James R Hill
Dept of Energy
PE-222
Washington, D.C.   20545

Eric Hilmer
Moore & Taber
1009 Fulton Av #118
Sacramento, CA   95813

Harry Himelblau
Space Trans Sys Dv Rockwell Intl
MC AB 97
Downey, CA   90241

Richard Hoar
TRW
PO Bx 1310
San Bernardino, CA   92402

Mr John F Holmes
State of Arizona
Facilities Plning Off. 604 W Wing
Phoenix, AZ   85007

Mr Stephen Hom
EQE, Inc
121 Second St-4th Floor
San Francisco, CA   94105

Mr William C Honeck
Forell/Elsesser Engineers, Inc.
539 Bryant Street
San Francisco, CA   94107

Mr George F Horowitz
The Metro. Water Dist. of So. Cal.
1111 Sunset Blvd. - P.O. Box 54153
Los Angeles, CA   90054

Prof George W Housner
Calif. Institute of Technology
211 Thomas Laboratory
Pasadena, CA   91125

Dr Carl C Hsieh
Cal Poly State University
1730 Jalisco Court
San Luis Obispo, CA   93401

Dr Moh-Jiann Huang
Dept. of Civil Eng. Univ. of CO Denv
1100 14 Street
Denver, CO   80202

Dr Donald E Hudson
IAEE
531 Vaquero Road
Arcadia, CA   91006

Dr Paul L Hummel
Univ. of Hawaii
Dept. of Civil Engineering
Honolulu, HA   96822

Dr Howard H Hwang
Brookhaven National Laboratory
60 Cornell Ave.
Upton, NY   11973

Mr Katsuya Igarashi
Kajima Corp
743 Everett St
El Cerrito, CA   94530

Roy A Imbsen
Engr Comp Corp
3217 Ramos Circle
Sacramento, CA   95827

Dr. Jeremy Isenberg
Weidlinger Assoc.
3000 Sand Hill Rd, Bldg 4, Ste 155
Menlo Park, CA   94025

Ms Margaret G Hopper

P.O. Box 1106
Golden, CO   80402

Mr Ko Hosakawa
Chiyoda Chem Engr & Cons Co
c/o Dames & Moore 500 Sansome St
San Francisco, CA   94111

Dr H.J. Hovland
PG&E
77 Beale St. Rm. 2631
San Francisco, CA   94106

Dr David P Hu
SD G&E
101 Ash St
San Diego, CA   92101

Mr Harry Hudak
TRA Architects
215 Columbia
Seattle, WA   98104

James Huffman
Lewis & Clark Law Sch
10015 SW Terwilliger Blvd
Portland, OR   97219

Dr Raul Husid
Shell Oil Co
6210 Hummingbird
Houston, TX   77096

Tze-How Hwang
Sargent & Lundy
5701 N. Sheridan Rd 11-G
Chicago, IL   60660

T Igusa
URS/Blume
130 Jessie St
San Francisco, CA   91304

Jack T Irick
Exxon Co USA
PO Bx 2189
Houston, TX   77001

Prof Isao Ishibashi
Cornell University
School of Civil & Envir. Engr.
Ithaca, NY   14853

Prof Wilfred D Iwan
Calif Inst of Tech
1201 E Calif Blvd, Mail Code 104-44
Pasadena, CA   91125

Dr Dharapuram S Jagannathan
Bechtel Power Corp.
12400 E. Imperial Hwy.
Norwalk, CA   90650

Dr J. C Jeing
URS/John A. Blume & Assoc.
130 Jessie St.
San Francisco, CA   94105

Mr Donald K Jephcott
Calif Office of State Archit.
9191 Rolling Tree Lane
Fair Oaks, CA   95628

Mr Milind R Joglekar
Univ of Texas
Dept of Civil Eng
Austin, TX   78712

Lililee Johnson
Rockwell Intl
8710 Holly Way
Buena Park, CA   90620

Dr Paul R Johnston
Failure Analysis Associates
2225 E. Bayshore Road
Palo Alto, CA   94303

Mr Michael S Johnstone
Nought-Six, Inc.
5917 Almaden Lane
Oakland, CA   94611

Mr Jeff Jones
Cty Walnut Creek Comm Dvlp Dpt
1666 North Main St
Walnut Creek, CA   94596

Mr Mark G Jones
Mark Tech Corp
333 Hayes St
San Francisco, CA   94102

Dr Yan Y Kagan

IGPP UCLA
Los Angeles, CA   90024

Dr Klaus H Jacob
Columbia Univ
Lamont-Doherty Geol Observ
Palisades, NY   10964

L James
Seismic Engr Assn
1300 Fourth St
Santa Monica, CA   90274

Prof Paul C Jennings
California Institute Of Technology
Cal Inst Tech Mail Code 104-44
Pasadena, CA   91125

Prof James O Jirsa
Ferguson Structural Engr. Lab.
Univ. of Texas, BRC
Austin, TX   78759

Mr Carl B Johnson
Johnson & Nielsen Assoc.
7462 N. Figueroa St.
Los Angeles, CA   90041

Mr William S Johnson

714-1/2 17th St.
Sacramento, CA   95814

Mr Roy G Johnston
Brandow & Johnston Assoc.
1660 West Third St.
Los Angeles, CA   90017

Dr. Barclay G Jones
Cornell Univ.
109 W Sibley(D of City & Reg Plan)
Ithaca, NY   14853

Dr Lindsay R Jones
Computech Engineering Services
2855 Telegraph Avenue, Suite 410
Berkeley, CA   94705

Dr William B Joyner
USGS
345 Middlefield Road
Menlo Park, CA   94025

Dr Takaaki Kagawa
McClelland Engr Inc
6100 Hillcroft
Houston, TX   77077

Dr Hasan Kamil
Engineering Decision Analysis Co. In
480 California Ave. Suite 301
Palo Alto, CA   94306

Rakesh K Kapania
Purdue Univ
Sch of Aero & Astro Grissom Hl
West Lafatette, IN   47907

Dr Dimitris L Karabalis
Ohio St Univ
470 Hitchcock Hall-2070 Neil Av
Columbus, OH   43210

Mr Michael K Kasamoto
Hawaii Structural Engineers
1326 Keeaumoku St. #602
Honolulu, HA   96814

Prof Edward Kavazanjian
Stanford Univ.
Dept of Civil Eng, Terman Eng Cntr
Stanford, CA   94305

Mr Eric L Keen
Advanced Engr
11941 Mary Ave
Anchorage, AK   99515

Mr Roger M Kenneally
U.S. Nuclear Reg. Comm.
Mail Stop 5650 NL
Washington, D.C.   20555

Dr Robert P Kennedy
Structural Mechanics Associates
5160 Birch St.
Newport Beach, CA   92660

Jeffrey K Kimball
US NRC
Mail Stop P-514
Washington, D.C.   20555

Prof Owen M Kirkley
Virginia Military Institute
203 W. Preston St.
Lexington, VA   24450

Mr. David E Kleiner
Harza Engineering Co.
150 S. Wacker Dr.
Chicago, IL   60606

Dr Daniel D Kana
Southwest Rsrch Inst
6220 Culebra Rd
San Antonio, TX   78284

Mr Larry R Kaprielian
Martin & Tranbarger
2210 Newport Blvd
Newport Beach, CA   92663

Mr Kazuhiko Kasai
UC Berkeley
2535 College Avenue #307
Berkeley, CA   94704

Prof Edward Kausel
MIT
Rm 1-271
Cambridge, MA   62139

Prof Makoto Kawamura
Cornell Univ
Sch Cvl Eng & Env Eng Hollstr Hl
Ithaca, NY   14853

Prof James M Kelly
University of California
Dept. of Civl Engineering
Berkeley, CA   94720

Mr James C Kennedy
The Hartford Ins Group
650 California St
San Francisco, CA   94111

Dr Mehran Keshavarzian
Walter P. Moore & Associates
2905 Sackett St.
Houston, TX   77098

Prof Anne S Kiremidjian
Stanford University
Terman Eng. Center
Stanford, CA   9430?

Dr Masaru Kitaura
Columbia University
610 S. W. Mudd Bldg.
New York, NY   10027

Mr George C Klimkiewicz
Weston Geophysical Corp
PO Bx 550 Lyons St
Westboro, MA   01581

Prof Richard E Klingner
Univ. of Texas
Dept. of Eng. ECJ 4.2
Austin, TX   78759

Mr William J Kockelman
USGS
345 Middlefield Road, MS 22
Menlo Park, CA   94025

Aik-Siong Koh
Univ of Texas
Dpt ASE/EM U. Texas
Austin, TX   78712-1085

Mr Henry T Krasodomski
G.E. Knolls Atomic Power Laboratory
P.O. Box 1072
Schenectady, NY   12309

Dr Michael E Kreger
Univ. of Texas at Austin
10100 Burnet Rd. #24 F.S.E. Lab
Austin, TX   78758

Mr Benjamin I Kron
Tennessee Valley Authority
400 Summit Hill 1112IBM-K
Knoxville, TN   37902

Mr Paul F Krumpe
Off. of Foreign Dis. Ag. For Int'l D
Rm 1262-A Dept. of State
Washington, D.C.   20523

Dr Shyh-Yuan Kung
Applied Research Associates
2101 San Pedro Blvd. NE, Suite A
Alburquerque, NM   87110

Prof Henry J Lagorio
Univ. Of California
C.E.D.R. 10 Donald Dr
Orinda, CA   94563

Mr Patrick J Lama
Mason Industries Inc.
708 N. Valley St. Suite K
Anaheim, CA   92801

Dr Richard A Larder
Larder Research & Development
655 Chetwood St, #401
Oakland, CA   94610

Mr K M Kluver
Portland Cement Assoc
83 Ryegate Place
San Ramon, CA   94583

Mr Subbarao V Kodavatiganti
Off Of Emergency Services
St. Of Ca. P.O.Box 9577
Sacramento, CA   95823

Dr Christian A Kot
Argonne Nat Lab
9700 S. Cass Av Bld 335
Argonne, IL   60439

Prof Helmut Krawinkler
Stanford Univ.
Dept. of Civil Eng.
Stanford, CA   94022

Dr Ellis L Krinitzsky
Waterways Experiment Station
P. O. Box 631
Vicksburg, MS   39180

Mr Alan Kropp
Alan Kropp & Assoc
2054 Univ Ave Ste 600
Berkeley, CA   94704

Dr Ram B Kulkarni
Woodward-Clyde Cons
1 Walnut Cr Cntr 100 Pringle Ave
Walnut Creek, CA   94596

Dr Onder Kustu
Consulting Engineer
555 Pierce St. # 420
Albany, CA   94706

Dr Paul C Lam
Univ of Akron
Dpt Mech Engr
Akron, OH   44325

Mr James F Lander
Nat'l Geophysical Data Ctr.
NOAA/EGC 315 Broadway
Boulder, CO   80302

F Lau
Skidmore Owings & Merrill
70 Universal City Plaza
Universal City, CA   91608

F. Lee
Shapiro, Okino, Hom & Assoc.
1736 Stockton St.
San Francisco, CA   94133

T.H. Lee
THL Intl Engr Cons Inc
3335 Willard St
San Diego, CA   92122

Mr David J Leeds
David J. Leeds & Assoc.
11972 Chalon Rd.
Los Angeles, CA   90049

John S Leiss
Fed ERC
825 N Capitol St
Washington, D.C.   20426

Mr Michael S Leonard
ABAM Engineers, Inc.
500 S. 336 St.
Federal Way, WA   98003

Ming B Leung
Exxon Production Rsrch Co
PO Bx 2189
Houston, TX   77001

Mr Murray Levish
Earth Systems Consultants
1900 Embarcadero Road, Suite 200
Palo Alto, CA   94303

Tingley K Lew
Naval Cvl Engr Lab
Port Hueneme
Ventura, CA   93043

Dr Albert N Lin
T.W. Lin Engineers
3323 Bryant Street
Palo Alto, CA   94306

Prof Y K Lin
Florida Atlantic Univ

Boca Raton, FL   33431

Dr Charles Lindbergh
Dept of Civil Engt
The Citadel
Charleston, SC   29409

Mr Peter L Lee
Skidmore, Ownings & Merrill
1 Maritime Plaza
San Francisco, CA   94104

Prof Vincent W Lee
Univ of S. Calif
Cvl Engr Dept,USC
Los Angeles, CA   90089-0242

Mr Mark R Legg
NTS/Wiggins Co
1650 South Pacific Coast Hwy
Redondo Beach, CA   90277

Prof Roberto Leon
Univ. of Minnesota
Dpt Cvl & Mnrl Eng 500 Pillsbury Dr
Minneapolis, MN   55455

Mr Milton G Leong
Leong/Razzano & Assoc Inc
366 40th ST
Oakland, CA   94609

Mr John T Levesque
SWRB Inc.
9823 44Th Avenue, S.W.
Seattle, WA   98136

Dr Marshall Lew
LeRoy Crandall & Associates
711 North Alvarado Street
Los Angeles, CA   90026-4099

Mr James E Ley
Department of Water Resources
5309 Mustang Way
Carmichael, CA   95608

Chi-Wen ' Lin
Westinghouse
PO Bx 355
Pittsburgh, PA   15230

Dr Herbert E Lindberg
SRI International
333 Ravenswood Ave.
Menlo Park, CA   94025

Russell L Lindbergh
Dpt Cvl Engr
Citadel
Charlston, SC   29409

Mr C. E Lindvall
Lindvall, Richter & Assoc.
815 Colorado Blvd.
Los Angeles, CA   90041

Dr Frederick C Lindvall
Lindvall, Richter & Assoc
815 Colorado Blvd.
Los Angeles, CA   90041

Mr Samuel J Linn, Jr.
State of California - DWR
6021 41st Street
Sacramento, CA   95824

Lon Lister
FERC
825 No Capitol St
Washington, D.C.   20426

J Litehiser
Bechtel
PO Bx 3965
San Francisco, CA   94119

S. C. Liu
National Science Foundation
705 Buccaneer Ct.
Silver Spring, MD   20904

Wen D Liu
Engr Comp Corp
3217 Ramos Circle
Sacramento, CA   95827

Mr Alfredo Lopez
Bechtel Power Corp.
135 Litchfield Ln.
Houston, TX   77024

Mr Gerardo A Lopez
Riley Stoker Corporation
P.O. Box 547
Worcester, MA   01613

Prof Shibo Lou

2822 Hillegass Ave
Berkeley, CA   94705

Samuel Louis
SC RTD
425 S. Main St
Los Angeles, CA   90013

Prof Le-Wu Lu
Lehigh University
Fritz Eng. Lab.
Bethlehem, PA   18015

Mr Clifford V Lucas
Calif. Dept. of Water Resources
1416 9th Street
Sacramento, CA   95814

Dr. Rene W Luft
Simpson Gumpertz & Heger
297 Broadway
Arlington, MA   02174

Mr. LeVal Lund
Water & Power
3245 Lowry Rd.
Los Angeles, CA   90027

Prof Loren D Lutes
Rice University
Dept. of Civil Engr. P. O. Box 1892
Houston, TX   77251

Ms Rhonda L MacDonald
C F Braun & Co
1700 Mission St #1
South Pasadena, CA   91030

John Macchi
Macchi Engrs
44 Gillett St
Hartford, CT   06105

Mr Stephen H Macie
Macie Engineering
849 Monterey Street
San Luis Obispo, CA   93401

George Mader
Wm Spangle & Assoc
3240 Albine Rd
Portola Valley, CA   94025

Stephen A Mahin
Univ of Calif
806 Highbridge Lane
Danville, CA   94526

Mr Richard P Maley
USGS
345 Middlefield Road
Menlo Park, CA   94025

Mr Shahrokh Manuchehri
CalTrans
150 Oak St
San Francisco, CA   94102

Dr Kenneth M Mark
Bechtel National, Inc.
50 Beale St.
San Francisco, CA   94105

Mr Hank Martin
American Iron & Steel Inst.
22932 El Toro Rd. #4
El Toro, CA   92630

Mr Stan Martin
LTV Energy Products Co
PO Bx BPD
Athens, TX   75751

Mr George H Matsumura
U.S. Army Corps of Engrs.
HQ USACE (DAEN-ECE-DS)
Washington, D.C.   20314

Mr Richard A Mayes
USKH Inc.
2515 'A' Street
Anchorage, AK   99503

Mr Frank E McClure
Lawrence Berkeley Lab
1 Cyclotron Rd
Berkeley, CA   94720

Mr Peter W McDonough
Mountain Fuel Supply Co.
1078 West First South St.
Salt Lake City, UT   84139

Dr Robin K McGuire
Dames & Moore
1262 Cole Blvd
Golden, CO   80401

Francis G McLean
US Bureau Of Reclam
PO Bx 25007
Denver, CO   80225

Prof Hugh D McNiven
University of California

Berkeley, CA   94720

Dr N.Dean Marachi
Converse Consultants
110 Bando Court
Walnut Creek, CA   94595

Dr Geoffrey R Martin
The Earth Technology Corp.
3777 Long Beach Blvd.
Long Beach, CA   90807

Mr Robert C Martin
Robert C. Martin
422 Green Glen Way
Mill Valley, CA   94941

Prof Sami F Masri
Univ Southern Calif
Cvl Engin Dept USC
Los Angeles, CA   90089-0242

Dr Gerald W May
College of Engineering
Univ of New Mexico
Albuquerque, NM   87131

Mr James E McCarty

5 Spyglass Hill
Oakland, CA   94618

Dr Richard D McConnell
Veterans Admin
C.E.S. (085) 811 Vermont Ave NW
Washington, D.C.   20420

Mr Charles H McElroy
Soil Conserv Service
POBX 6567
Fort Worth, TX   76115

Prof William McGuire
Cornell University
School of Civil Engr.
Ithaca, NY   14850

Mr Douglas K McLeod
Arctic Designers
P. O. Box 82190
Fairbanks, AK   99708

Mr Ronald P Mcrobbie
Air Force Reg Cvl Engr
630 Sansome St
San Fransico, CA   94960

Mr Terrance S Meade
FEMA Region IX
Building 105 Presidio
San Francisco, CA 94129

Mr John F Meehan
Structural Safety Section
671 Laurel Drive
Sacramento, CA 95825

Mr Les C Melhorn
CH2M Hill
2200 Powell Street, 8th Fl.
Emeryville, CA 94608

Dr Howard C Merchant
MerEnCo Inc
9 Lake Bellevue Dr
Bellevue, WA 98005

Prof Christian Meyer
Columbia Univ
Dept Cvl Engr
New York, NY 10027

Mr Ronald F Middlebrook
Martin, Middlebrook, Nishkian
111 Townsend St
San Francisco, CA 94107

Charles A Miller
City College NY
8 Hastings Rd
Monsey, NY 10912

Prof Russell S Mills
Div of Engr CSU
Chico St Univ
Chico, CA 95929-930

Mr Akira Mita

7405 Armstrong Pl #B-21
San Diego, CA 92111

Mr Takashi Mochio
Columbia Univ.
640 Mudd Bldg. Columbia Univ.
New York, NY 10027

Dr A.Q. Mohammad
Pratt Inst
174 Emerson Pl Sch Engr
Brooklyn, NY 11205

Mr Ronald W Mearns
City of San Jose
801 N. First St. Room 340
San Jose, CA 95110

Dr Lelio H Mejia
Harding Lawson Assoc.
666 Howard St.
San Francisco, CA 94105

Mr Stanley H Mendes
Stanley H Mendes Inc
3757 State St., Suite 201
Santa Barbara, CA 93105

Dr Joshua L Merritt
Merritt CASES Inc
710 Brookside Av Ste 3/PO Bx 1206
Redlands, CA 92373

Mr Anthony D Meyers
GW Consulting Engrs
2700 Glendale Lane
Sacramento, CA 95825

Ms Isabella Z Mika
Powell, Mika And Associates
141 S. Lake Ave., Suite 120
Pasadena, CA 91101

Prof Richard K Miller
Univ Southern Calif
Cvl Engr Dept USC
Los Angeles, CA 90089-0242

Mr Ravindra P Mistry

3531 Skyline Drive
Hayward, CA 94542

Mr Warren W Mitchell
Chevron Corp
Rm 1400 555 Market St
San Francisco, CA 94105-2870

Jack P Moehle
Univ of Calif
714 Davis Hall
Berkeley, CA 94706

Dr Piotr D Moncarz
Failure Analysis Associates
2225 East Bayshore Rd
Palo Alto, CA 94303

Mr Neil J Monroe
The Babcock & Wilcox Co.
4282 Strausser St. N.W.
North Canton, OH   44720

Tom Moore
Integrated Design
1685 Suncrest Ct
Walnut Creek, CA   94596

Mr Ugo Morelli
Federal Emergency Management Agency
500 C. Street S.W.
Washington, D.C.   20472

Dr Naser Mostagnhel
Univ of Utah
Dept of Civil Engr,3012 MEB
Salt Lake City, UT   84112

Dr Peter Mueller
Lehigh Univ
Lehigh U. Fritz Engr Lab #13
Bethlehem, PA   18015

Dr Andrew J Murphy
U.S. Nuclear Reg. Comm
Mail Stop 1130-SS
Washington, D.C.   20555

Dr Farzad Naeim
John A. Martin & Assoc.
1800 Wilshire Boulevard
Los Angeles, CA   90057

Robert Nason
USGS
345 Middlefield
Menlo Park, CA   94025

Mr Soheil Nazarian
Univ of Texas, Austin
Dept of Cvl Engr, ECJ 6.3
Austin, TX   78712

Mrs Dorothy S Ng
Lawrence Livermore Nat Lab
PO Bx 1155
Livermore, CA   94550

Mr Robert Nichelini
City of Oakland
455 7th St
Oakland, CA   94607

Ms Gwendolyn B Moore
Cosmos Corporation
1730 K St., N.W., Suite 1302
Washington, D.C.   20006

Mr William W Moore
Dames & Moore
500 Sansome Street
San Francisco, CA   94111

Mr Peter N Mork
USGS
345 Middlefield Road
Menlo Park, CA   94025

Lalliana Mualchin
CA Div of Mines & Geo
2815 O St
Sacramento, CA   95816

Mr Richard L Munoz
Bureau of Reclamation
PO Bx 25007
Denver, CO   80225

Dr Robert C Murray
Lawrence Livermore Lab
P.O. Box 808,L-390
Livermore, CA   94550

Prof William A Nash
Univ. of Massachusetts
Dept of Civil Eng(Marston Hall)
Amherst, MA   01003

Dr James M Nau
N.C. St Univ
Dept of Civil Engrs POBx 7908
Raleigh, NC   27695-7908

Mr Aly S Nazmy
Princeton Univ
Dpt Cvl Eng Princeton Univ
Princeton, NJ   08544

Mansour Niazi
Tera Corp
2150 Shattuck Ave
Berkeley, CA   94704

Mr John J Nicholl
MicroGeophysics Corp
10900 W 44th Av
Wheat Ridge, CO   80033

Mr Joseph P Nicoletti
URS/John A. Blume Assoc.
130 Jessie St
San Francisco, CA   94105

Mr Robert L Nigbor
Kinemetrics, Inc.
222 Vista Avenue
Pasadena, CA   91107

Mr David M Noguchi
Office of the State Architect
1500 5th Street
Sacramento, CA   95814

Mr Guy J Nordenson
Weidlinger Assoc.
333 Seventh Ave.
New York, NY   10001

Prof Andrzej S Nowak
Univ of Michigan
W Engr Bldg Rm 312B
Ann Arbor, MI   48109

Mr Richard V Nutt
Applied Technology Council
2471 E. Bayshore Blvd. Suite 512
Palo Alto, CA   94303

Mr David W Nyby
CH2M Hill
2148 Park Marina Dr
Redding, CA   96001

Mr Ralph G Oesterle
Portland Cement Association
5420 Old Orchard Road
Skokie, IL   60077-4321

Tadahiko Okumura
Shimuzu Const Co Ltd
261 S. Figueroa St Ste 120
Los Angeles, CA   90012

Mr Bruce C Olsen
Bruce C. Olsen Consl. Engr.
1411 - 4th Avenue #1420
Seattle, WA   98101

Mr Richard S Olsen
Waterways Experiment Station
P. O. Box 631
Vicksburg, MS   39180

Dr Norby Nielsen
University of Hawaii
Civil Eng. 2540 Dole Street
Honolulu, HA   96822

Prof Toyoaki Nogami
University of Houston
Dept Civil Engr U.H., Univ Park
Houston, TX   77004

Dr James L Noland
Atkinson-Noland & Assoc.
2619 Spruce St
Boulder, CO   80302

Ms Linda L Nott
Structech
7454 No Flora St.
Fresno, CA   93710

Dr Michael J Nowak
U.S. International U.
10455 Pomerado Rd
San Diego, CA   92131

Prof Otto W Nuttli
Saint Louis University
P.O. Box 8099 Laclede Station
St. Louis, MO   63156

T.D. O'Rourke
Cornell Univ
265 Hollister Hall
Ithica, NY   14853

Mr Takao Okazaki
Taisei Corp.
1600 Center Ave., Apt. 2C
Fort Lee, NJ   07024

Prof Michael G Oliva
Univ of California
232 Wurster Hall Arch
Berkeley, CA   94720

Mr Irving E Olsen
Dames & Moore
17340 Canyon Dr
Lake Oswego, OR   97034

Mr Robert A Olson
VSP Assoc Inc
PO Bx 255325
Sacramento, CA   95865

Mr Masaru Onoe
Akashi Seisakusho
3255-6C Scott Blvd
Santa Clara, CA   95051

Mr Leonard M Osborne
L.A. Dept. of Water & Power
P.O. Box 111, Room 1314
Los Angeles, CA   90051

Dr Kenneth B Oster
University of Missouri-Rolla
G4B Engineering Mech. Bldg.
Rolla, MO   65401

Mr George E Pace
Air Force Regional Civil Engineer
11534 Anderson Street
Loma Linda, CA   92354

Dr Tso-Chien Pan
Advanced Tec/Bechtel
4640 Setting Sun Drive
El Sobrante, CA   94803

Gerard C Pardoen
Englekirk/Hart
2116 Arlington Ave
Los Angeles, CA   90018

Prof Richard A Parmelee
Northwestern University
Dept. Of Civil Eng. Tech Inst.
Evanston, IL   60201

Mr Stephen E Pauly
Kinemetrics
222 Vista Ave
Pasadena, CA   91107

Mr Wilfred W Peak
Private Consultant
6360 Eichler St.
Sacramento, CA   95831

Virgilio Perez
USGS
128 Woodland Ave
San Francisco, CA   94117

Mr Fred Petry
H.B.E. Corp
11330 Olive Blvd PO Bx 27339
St Louis, MO   63141

Dr Irving J Oppenheim
Carnegie-Mellon Univ
Dept. of Civil Engineering
Pittsburgh, PA   15213

Dr Farhang Ostadan
Earthquake Engineering Tech.
2400 Old Crow Canyon Road
San Ramon, CA   94583

Dr Norman G Owen
URS/Blume Engineers
130 Jessie St.
San Francisco, CA   94105

Dr Nick N Pal
Pal Consultants Inc
2797 Park Ave
Santa Clara, CA   95050

Mr Bernd Pankow
Riley Stoker Corp.
P.O. Box 547
Worcester, MA   01613

Lt Donald Parker
City of Oakland Fire Dept
1605 Grove St Firehouse #1
Oakland, CA   94612

Mr Goutam Paul
INTEL Corp
3200 Lakeside Dr SC6-621
Santa Clara, CA   95050

Dr Joy M Pauschke
University of Pennsylvania
113 Town Bldg-D3 Dpt Cvl Eng
Philadelphia, PA   19104

Prof Joseph Penzien
Univ. of Calif. Berkeley
Rm. 731 Davis Hall
Berkeley, CA   94720

Mr Vernon H Persson
Dept. of Water Resources
6217 Knollcrest Court
Carmichael, CA   95608

Bertold W Pfeifer
Bechtel Pwr Corp
50 Beale St
San Francisco, CA   94119

Dr Edward O Pfrang
American Soc Cvl Engr
345 East 47 St
New York, NY   10017

Michael P Piazza
Exxon Pro Rsrch Co
PO Bx 2189
Houston, TX   77001

Mr Gilberto F Pineda
Metropolitan Sanitary District
15312 S. Dobson Avenue
South Holland, IL   60473

Mr Clarkson W Pinkham
S.B. Barnes & Assoc.
2236 Beverly Blvd.
Los Angeles, CA   90057

Dr Jose A Pires
Brookhaven Nat Lab
Brookhaven Nat Lab Bld 129
Upton, NY   11973

Prof Karl S Pister
Univ. of California
College of Engineering
Berkeley, CA   94720

Mr Chris D Poland
H.J. Degenkolb Assoc
350 Sansome St #500
San Francisco, CA   94104

Eugenio Pollner
EERC U.C.
555 Pierce St #F 844
Albany, CA   94706

Mr Eltweed G Pomeroy
Caltrans-Structures Design
5050 Pomegranate Avenue
Sacramento, CA   95823

Mr Charles Poparad
Hilti Inc
4115 S. 100th E. Ave
Tulsa, OK   74146

Prof Egor P Popov
Univ. of California
Davis Hall
Berkeley, CA   94720

Dr Lawrence D Porter
Sohio Petroleum Co
PO Bx 915
Danville, CA   94526

Dr Max L Porter
Iowa State University
Civil Engrg. Dept.
Ames, IA   50011

Mr Allan R Porush
C. F. Braun & Co.
157 S. Hermosa Avenue
Sierra Madre, CA   91024

Maurice S Power
Woodward-Clyde Cons
One Walnut Creek Center
Walnut Creek, CA   94596

Michael Praszker
Lee Praszker
147 Natoma St
San Francisco, CA   94105

Mr Albert S Pratt
Pblc Wrks Dpt Pac Mis Tst Cntr
Code Pacific Missle Test Cntr
Point Mugu, CA   93042

Mr F. R Preece
Preece, Goudie & Assoc.
300 Montgomery St.
San Francisco, CA   94104

Dr James D Prendergast
U.S. Construction Eng. Res.
PO Bx 4005
Champaign, IL   61820

Dr. Frank Press
Nat Academy of Sciences
2101 Constitution Av NW
Washington, D.C.   20418

Ms Jane Preuss
Urban Regional Rsrch
616 1st St Suite 200
Seattle, WA   98104

Mr C W Price
North American Reinsurance Corp
100 E 46th St
New York, NY   10017

Mr Robert W Prindle
Sandia Nat Labs
PO Bx 5800-Div 6252
Albuquerque, NM   87185

Robert Pyke
TAGA Inc
2855 Telegraph Av #415
Berkeley, CA   94705

Dr Enrico L Quarantelli
Disaster Research Center
Derby Hall, Ohio State Univ.
Columbus, OH   43210

Melvin Ramey
Univ of Calif
Cvl Engr Dpt
Davis, CA   95616

Prof Ahmed A Rashed
The Johns Hopkins Univ
Dept Of Civil Eng, 34 & Charles
Baltimore, MD   21218

Dr M. Ravindra
NTS / Structural Mechanics
15 Fortuna West
Irvine, CA   92660

Dr Andrei Reinhorn
SUNY at Buffulo
Dept Cvl Engr-West Bldg
Buffalo, NY   14260

Gilbert J Reyes
Naval Fac Engr Cmnd
PO Bx 727 Code 411
San Bruno, CA   94066

Mr James A Richardson
Univ of Nevada Reno
Civil Engr Dpt
Reno, NV   89557

Dr Satwant S Rihal
Cal Poly St Univ
Architectural Engr Dept
San Luis Obispo, CA   93407

Mr John E Rinne

16 Yale Circle
Kensington, CA   94708

Mr Anthony Prud'homme
Atlantic Richfield Co.
515 So. Flower Street
Los Angeles, CA   90071

Mr Jianhua Qi
PRC
2708 College Ave #12
Berkeley, CA   94705

Dr James B Radziminski
Univ. of South Carolina
207 Engineering Building
Columbia, SC   29208

Dr Sridhar J Rao
California State University
13115 E. Espinheira Drive
Cerritos, CA   90701

Mr Gary S Rasmussen
Gary S. Rasmussen & Assoc Inc
1811 Commercenter W
San Bernardino, CA   92408

Charlés Real
CDMG
2815 O St
Sacramento, CA   95816

Robert Reitherman
SSI
517 E Bayshore Rd
Redwood City, CA   94019

Mr Philip E Reynolds
Pacific Gas Transmission Co.
245 Market St., Room 1408
San Francisco, CA   94105-1776

Mr Philip J Richter
Fluor Engineers Inc.
3333 Michelson Drive
Irvine, CA   92730

William Rihn
Kinemetrics Inc
222 Vista Ave
Pasadena, CA   91107

C.E. Rivero
U.T.A.
5809 Willow Crest Dr
Arlington, TX   76017

Paul Rizzo
Rizzo Assoc
PO Bx 17180
Pittsburgh, PA   15235

Dr Albert M Rogers
USGS
Den. Fed. Center, MS966
Denver, CO   80225

Ms Catherine Roha

1641 Allston Way
Berkeley, CA   94703

Mr J. H Rokita

271 Carolina Ln.
Palo Alto, CA   94306

Dr C L Ross
Georgia
City Planning Pgm Cllge of Arch
Atlanta, GA   30332

Dennis Row
SSD Inc
1930 Shattuck Ave
Berkeley, CA   94704

Mr James E Russell
City of Palo Alto
1236 Third Ave.
San Francisco, CA   94122

Mr Abdul-Rahim R Sabouni
Cornell Univ.
Hollister Hall
Ithaca, NY   14853

Dr Frederick B Safford
Agbabian Associates
250 N. Nash St.
El Segundo, CA   90245-0956

Mr Richard Sanchez
CA Dept. of Water Resources
P. O. Box 388
Sacramento, CA   95802

Prof Ranbir S Sandhu
Ohio State University
Dept of Civil Engr 2070 Neil Av
Columbus, OH   43210

Mr Alfred O Rock
Oshpd Div. Of Facilities Devel
1600 9Th Street, Room 410
Sacramento, CA   95628

Mr Kent R Rogers
Skilling Ward Rogers Barkshire
725 Greenwich, Suite 400
San Francisco, CA   94133

Mr Christopher Rojahn
Applied Technology Council
2471 E. Bayshore Rd, Suite 512
Palo Alto, CA   94301

Mr Steven C Roper
Wiss, Janney, Elstner Assoc.
2200 Powell St., Suite 925
Emeryville, CA   94608

Wolfgang Roth
Dames & Moore
445 Figueroa
Los Angeles, CA   90071

Mr Manlio Roy
Martin & Tranbarger
2210 Newport Blvd.
Newport Beach, CA   92663

Mr Francis J Russo
Federal Emergency Management Agency
500 C St. SW
Washington, D.C.   20472

Bahram Safavi
Stanford Univ
PO Bx 9290
Stanford, CA   94305

Prof Sven Sahlin
Univ. of Texas, Austin
8603 Azalea Trail
Austin, TX   78759

Mr Henry P Sanders
Wheeler & Gray, Cons Engrs
7462 North Figueroa St
Los Angeles, CA   90041

Mr Joseph R Santos
Calif. Dept. Water Res.
2520 Edam Street
Lancaster, CA   93534

Dr Mehdi Saoode
Univ of Nevada Reno
Civil Engr Dept
Reno, NV   89557

Mr Richard Sause
U.C. Berkeley- EERC
2703 Woolsey St. #2
Berkeley, CA   94705

Dr John B Scalzi
National Science Foundation
1800 G Street, Nw
Washington, D.C.   20550

Dr Charles Scawthorn
Dames & Moore
500 Sansome
San Francisco, CA   94111

Prof Anshel J Schiff
Purdue Univ
25 Pearce-Mitchell
Stanford, CA   94305

Dr Roger E Scholl
EERI & URS Blume Eng.
130 Jessie Street
San Franciso, CA   94105

Vahid Schricker
SSD Inc
1930 Shattuck Ave
Berkeley, CA   94704

David P Schwartz
Woodward Clyde Cons
100 Pringle Ave
Walnut Creek, CA   94596

Mr William M Seay
Tennessee Valley Authority
400 West Summit Hill Dr., 175 LB
Knoxville, TN   37902

Prof Harry B Seed
Univ. of California
Rm 441 Davis Hall U.C.
Berkeley, CA   94720

Prof Lawrence G Selna
UCLA
Dept. of Civil Engineering
Los Angeles, CA   90024

Mr Abrol C Satish
HQUSAF/LEEE
Bld #516 Bolling A.F.B.
Washington, D.C.   20332

William P Savage
SLAC
P. O. Box 4349
Stanford, CA   94305

Mr Raymond J Scaramella
Geotechnical Exploration, Inc.
8145 Ronson Road, Suite H
San Diego, CA   92111

Dr Charles F Scheffey
Federal Highway Admin.
6800 Georgetown Pike
McLean, VA   22101

Prof William C Schnobrich
Univ of Illinois
Dept. of Civil Eng, 208 N. Romine
Urbana, IL   61801

Mr Craig C Schoof
Failure Analysis Associates
2225 East Bayshore
Palo Alto, CA   94303

Mr Arie B Schuurman
PG&E
77 Beale St. C.E. Dept. Rm. 2621
San Francisco, CA   94106

Mr Stanley Scott
Univ. of Calif.
1141 Vallecito Ct.
Lafayette, CA   94549

Mr Girgis Y Sedra

58 E 11th Ave #32
Columbus, OH   43201

Prof Raymond B Seed
Stanford Univ.
Terman Engr Center
Stanford, CA   94305

Mr Kimihiro Sera
Structcon
1234 No Wishion
Fresno, CA   93728

Mr Manohar Sethi
Lawrence Livermore Nat'l Laboratory
P.O. Box 5506,L-799
Livermore, CA   94550

Dr Surendra P Shah
Northwestern Univ
Dept Cvl Engr
Evanston, IL   ·60201

Mr Paul J Shanta

2705 Gamble Ct.
Hayward, CA   94542

Mr Ram P Sharma
International Engr Co
180 Howard St.
San Francisco, CA   94105

Dr Shamim A Sheikh
University Of Houston
Dept. Of Civil Engineering
Houston, TX   77004

Li-Hong Sheng
CalTrans
PO Bx 1499
Sacramento, CA   95807

Ruth Sheshinski
Hebrew Univ Of Jerusalem
Dp Statistics Stanford Univ
Stanford, CA   94305

Mr Kazushi Shimazaki
Univ of Illinois
3105 NCEL, Univ of IL
Urbana, IL   61801

Prof Masanobu Shinozuka
Columbia University
Dpt Cvl Eng 610 SW Mudd 520W120St
New York, NY   10025

Mr K. N Shiu
Portland Cement Assoc.
5420 Old Orchard Rd.
Skokie, IL   60077

Ms Lisa M Shusto
Failure Analysis Associates
2225 E. Bayshore Road
Palo Alto, CA   94303

Prof Haresh C Shah
Stanford University
Dept. of Civil Engineering
Stanford, CA   94305

Dr Anthony F Shakal
CDMG/SMIP
2811 O St
Sacramento, CA   95816

Mr Mohan P Sharma

Rm 544 Blume Center
Stanford, CA   94305

Mr Roland L Sharpe
Engineering Decision Analysis Co.
480 California Ave. #301
Palo Alto, CA   94306

Prof C.K. Shen
Univ. of California, Davis
Dept of Civil Eng.
Davis, CA   95616

Roger W Sherburne
Calif Div Mines & Geo
2811 O St
Sacramento, CA   95816

Mr Ramkishan V Shetty
EBASCO Services Inc.
P. O. Box 1189
Elma, WA   98503

Dr Pui-Shum B Shing
U.C. Berkeley
2390 Parker St Apt 9
Berkeley, CA   94704

Mr. Takeshi Shirasuna
Ohbayashi-Gumi, Ltd.
333 Shenandoah Circle
Blacksburg, VA   24060

Edwin Shlemon
Skidmor Owings Merrill
1675 Broadway Suite 400
Denver, CO   80111

Mr George B Sigal
Burns & Roe Inc
800 Kinder Kamack Rd
Oradell, NJ   07649

JP Singh
Harding Lawson Assoc
7655 Redwood Blvd
Novato, CA   94947

M.P. Singh
VA Tech
608 Piedmont St
Blacksburg, VA   24060

Mr Tony X Sison
R.W. Beck and Assoc
Tower Bldg 7th Ave
Seattle, WA   98101

Mr Mitch Smith
Hilti Inc
14500 Doolittle Dr
San Leandro, CA   94577

Mr Gary M Snyder
The Metro. Water Dist. of So. Cal.
1111 Sunset Blvd. - P.O. Box 54154
Los Angeles, CA   90054

Dr Norman F Somes
Bechtel Group Inc.
50 Beale St Bx3965 MlStop 50/4/A-6
San Francisco, CA   94119

Prof Abe H Soni
Oklahoma St Univ
Sch Mech Aero Eng EN 218
Stillwater, OK   74078

Mr Vahid Sotoudeh
Stanford University
P. O. Box 6171
Stanford, CA   94305

Mr Mete A Sozen
Univ. Illinois
3112 Newmark, 208 N. Romine
Urbana, IL   61801

Mr William E Spangle
William Spangle & Assoc. Inc.
3240 Alpine Rd.
Portola Valley, CA   94025

Mr Carl Sramek
Holmes & Narver, Inc.
2912 Inverness Dr.
Los Alamitos, CA   90720

Mr Jag N Singh
EG&G Idaho, Inc.
1955 Fremont Ave., P.O. Box 1625
Idaho Falls, ID   83415

Prof Avinash C Singhal
Arizona St Univ
Dept of Civil Engr
Tempe, AZ   85287

Dr David B Slemmons
Univ Of Nevada
2995 Golden Valley Rd
Reno, NV   89506

Mr Frederic G Snider
Ebasco Services Inc
2211 W. Meadowview Rd.
Greensboro, NC   27407

Dr Lawrence A Soltis
Forest Products Laboratory
P. O. Box 5130
Madison, WI   53705

Mr Steven A Sommers
Ohio State Univ.
2070 Neil Ave. Dept. of Civil Eng
Columbus, OH   43210

Steve Soo
City Of San Francisco
45 Hyde St
San Francisco, CA   94102

Dr Cetin Soydemir
Haley & Aldrich, Inc
238 Main St.
Cambridge, MA   01242

Mr Alan W Spang
Geocon Inc.
9530 Dowdy Dr.
San Diego, CA   92126

Dr Paul A Spudich
USGS
345 Middlefield Road
Menlo Park, CA   94025

Dr Muthukrishnan G Srinivasan
Argonne National Laboratory
9700 S. Cass, Bldg. 335
Argonne, IL   60516

Mr Hrista Stamenkovic
City Of Riverside
4426 Twelfth Street
Riverside, CA   92501

Mr Charles E Stearns
Soil Conservation Service
511 NW Broadway Rm. 514
Portland, OR   97209

Mr Raymond E Steinberg
Raymond Steinberg and Assoc.
14416 Victory Bl #107
Van Nuys, CA   91401

Mr Otto W Steinhardt
PG&E
45 Fremont, 23rd Floor
San Francisco, CA   94106

Mr Malcolm N Stephens
California Dept. of Water Resources
P. O. Box 488
Sacramento, CA   95802

J C Stepp
EPRI
3412 Hillview Ave
Palo Alto, CA   94303

Jerry Stockbridge
WJE Assoc
330 Pfingsten Rd
Northbrook, IL   60062

Mr James L Stratta
James Stratta Conslt Engr
3000 Sand Hill Rd Bld 4 Suite 110
Menlo Park, CA   94025

Mr Edward J Stuber
Associated Pile & Fitting Corp.
1750 Taylor St, Suite 1102
San Francisco, CA   94133

Dr Robert H Sues
Structural Mechanics Associates
5160 Birch St.
Newport Beach, CA   92660

Mr Saravanapavananthan Sutharshana
Cornell Univ
School Civil Engr, Cornell U.
Ithaca, NY   14853

Prof John F Stanton
University Of Washington
Dept. Of Civil Eng., Fx-10
Seattle, WA   98102

Mr Randolph E Steen
Parsons Brinckerhoff Inc
1510 Arden Way Suite 301
Sacramento, CA   95815

Mr Karl V Steinbrugge

6851 Cutting Blvd.
El Cerrito, CA   94530

Mr John R Stellar
Converse Consultants, Inc.
126 W Del Mar Blvd
Pasadena, CA   91105

Vince M Stephens
Robert Cloud and Assoc
125 Univ Ave
Berkeley, CA   94710

John D Stevenson
Stevenson & Assoc
9217 Midwest Ave
Cleveland, OH   44122

Prof Kenneth H Stokoe
Univ of Texas, Austin
Dept of Cvl Engr ECJ 6.3
Austin, TX   78712

Mr Thomas W Stratton,Jr.
East Bay MUD
P.O. Box 24055
Oakland, CA   94623

Dr Hon H Su
California State Univ.
6000 J Street
Sacramento, CA   95628

Dr Chang-Ning Sun
Tennessee Valley Authority
400 Summit Hill Dr., West 156,Lb-K
Knoxville, TN   37902

Ro Marjorie S Swain
Kinemetrics
222 Vista Ave
Pasadena, CA   91107

Mr Robert F Swalley
Swalley Engineering
1815 State St. Suite C.
Santa Barbara, CA   93101

Mr James C Tai
T.Y. Lin Intl.
315 Bay St.
San Francisco, CA   94133

Armen Tajirian

2722 Adeline St
Oakland, CA   94607

Hidehiro Takai
Hazama-gumi Ltd
560 Intl House 2299 Piedmont
Berkeley, CA   94720

Mr Louie H Tan
City Of Anaheim, Bldg. Divi.
200 S. Anaheim Blvd.
Anaheim, CA   92805

Mr James Tanouye
US Army Corps of Engineers
630 Sansome
San Francisco, CA   94111

Dr Alexander G Tarics
Reid And Tarics Assoc
20 Jones St
San Francisco, CA   94102

Mr Tom Tejima
TransPacific Geotech Engrs
611 Vetrans Blvd Suite 213
Redwood City, CA   94063

Dr. Charles C Thiel Jr.
Telesis Consultants
365 San Carlos
Piedmont, CA   94611

Dr James B Thompson
GeoEngineers, Inc.
P. O. Box 6325
Bellevue, WA   98008

Mr David D Tillson
S-Cubed
530 11th Avenue
Salt Lake City, UT   84103

Mr Daniel W Symonds
KPFF Cons Engr
700 Lloyd Bldg
Seattle, WA   98101

Richard G Tait
Harlan Miller Tait Assoc
1110 Van Ness Ave S
San Francisco, CA   94109

Stanley K Takahashi
Naval Cvl Engr Lab

Oxnard, CA   93043

Mr Dennis Y Tam
City of San Jose
801 N. First St., Room 300
San Jose, CA   95110

H.T. Tang
EPRI
3412 Hillview Ave
Palo Alto, CA   94303

Mr Xuekang Tao
Chinese Academy of Bldg Research
N. Hawkins 201 More H FX-10 U Wash
Seattle, WA   98195

Mr James R Teevan
Teevan Co
1840 Washington St
San Francisco, CA   94109

Mr Robert E Tepel
Santa Clara Valley Water District
5750 Almaden Expressway
San Jose, CA   95118

Mr Eugene W Thomas
Bechtel Power Corp
15740 Shady Grove Rd
Gaithersburg, MD   20877-1454

Mr Norman R Tilford
Ebasco Services Inc.
2211 W. Meadowview Rd.
Greensboro, NC   27407

Dr Ricardo A Todeschini
Bechtel Group Inc
50 Beale St POBx 3965
San Francisco, CA   94119

Dr Kohji Tokimatsu
Univ. of California
472 Davis Hall
Berkeley, CA   94720

Prof Mihailo D Trifunac
Univ Southern Cal
DRB 384 USC
Los Angeles, CA   90089-1114

Mr Kevin Z Truman
Washington Univ. Dept. of C.E.
Lindell & Skinker
St. Louis, MO   63130

Dr Wen S Tseng
Bechtel Power Corp.
50 Beale St., P.O.Box 3695
San Francisco, CA   94119

Brian E Tucker
Calif Div Mines Geo
2815 O St
Sacramento, CA   95816

Mr John B Tulloch
Eeri-Tulloch Construction
3428 Ettie Street
Oakland, CA   94608

F.E. Udwadia
USC
364 DRB Univ Park
Los Angeles, CA   90007

Dr Julio E Valera
Earth Sciences Assoc.
701 Welch Road
Palo Alto, CA   94304

Norman Van Dine
Sanders Assoc Inc
Grenier Field
Manchester, NH   03103

Prof Erik H Vanmarcke
MIT
Rm 1-238 MIT
Cambridge, MA   01239

Prof Anestis S Veletsos
Rice Univ
Dpt Cvl Eng Rice Univ
Houston, TX   77251

Mr Leslie V Tonkin
Tonkin/Greissinger Architects
801 1st Ave S
Seattle, WA   98134

Mr Paul Troutner
City Of Stockton
6 East Lindsay Street
Stockton, CA   95202

Dr (Tom) N.C. Tsai
NCT Engineering
P. O. Box 1937
Lafayette, CA   94556

Prof Kentaro Tsutsumi
Tufts Univ
Anderson Hall
Medford, MA   02155

Alice Tulloch
OKJ
2071 Cedar Crest
Merced, CA   95340

Mr Paul M Turkheimer
Wyle Laboratories
128 Maryland St.
El Segundo, CA   90245

Dr Jorge B Valdivieso
Brown & Root Inc.
4100 Clinton Drive
Houston, TX   77020-6299

Jose Vallenas
Cygna
101 California
San Francisco, CA   94111

Mr Gary E Van Houten
Van Houten Consultants
320 Washington Street
Petaluma, CA   94952

Mr Jim Vaughn
MCI Telecommunications
15303 Ventura Suite 300
Sherman Oaks, CA   91403

Marco Venturino
West Div Navfac
Box 727
San Bruno, CA   94010

Mr Andy Viksne
U.S. Bureau Of Reclamation
(Code 1631) P.O. Box 25007
Denver, CO   80225

Dr Ajit S Virdee
CSU Sac Dept Civil Engr
420 Broadway
Sacramento, CA   95818

Ms Maryann T Wagner
H.J. Degenkolb Assoc
350 Sansome St #500
San Francisco, CA   94104

Mr Howard H Waldron
Shannon & Wilson, Inc.
1105 NO. 38 St.
Seattle, WA   98103

Dr Robert E Wallace
USGS
345 Middlefield Road
Menlo Park, CA   94025

Ms Marcy L Wang
U.C. Berkeley
1096 Miller Ave.
Berkeley, CA   94708

Mr C N Watry
Watry Engineering Inc
2000 Broadway St 200
Redwood City, CA   94063

Dr Fred A Webster
JBA Inc
511 Bay Rd
Menlo Park, CA   94025

Prof Yi-Kwei Wen
Univ. of Illinois
Dept. of Civil Eng., 208 N Romine
Urbana, IL   61801

Mr Stuart D Werner
Agbabian Associates
250 N Nash
El Segundo, CA   90245

Rich White
Cornell U.
Hollister Hall
Ithaca, NY   14853

Prof Roberto Villaverde
Univ of Calif, Irvine
Dept of Civil Engr
Irvine, CA   92714

Mr John Vrymoed
CalTrans
1120 N St
Sacramento, CA   95814

Ms Vicki Wagner
Vicki Wagner, Consulting Engr.
1115 Underhills Road
Oakland, CA   94610

Mr Benjamin J Wallace
Stanford Univ
2921 Waverley St
Palo Alto, CA   94306

Leon R Wang
Univ of OK
Sch Cvl Engr Env Sci
Norman, OK   73019

Mr James Warner
Consulting Engineer
P.O. Box 1208
Mariposa, CA   95338

Mr. H. D Webber
L.T.V. Energy Products Co.
P.O. BxBPD
Athens, TX   75751

Mr Stephen M Weissberg
GSA-Design & Construction
525 Market Street, 9PC
San Francisco, CA   94105

Mr W. A Wenger, Jr.
John Brown Eng. & Const. Inc.
P. O. Box 720421
Houston, TX   77272

Dr. Bruce D Westermo
San Diego State Univ.
Dept. of Civil Eng.
San Diego, CA   92182-0189

Dr William H White
Bechtel Power Corp.
50 Beale Street (45/23/B34)
San Francisco, CA   94105

Prof Robert V Whitman
MIT
Room 1-342 MIT
Cambridge, MA   02139

Prof James K Wight
Univ. of Michigan
Dept. of Civil Engineering
Ann Arbor, MI   48109

Brian Wilson
PMB Systems Engin
500 Sansome St
San Francisco, CA   94111

Robert Wilson
7EMA
500 C St SW Rm 418
Washington, D.C.   20013

Mr Joel M Wolf
Failure Analysis Assoc.
2225 East Bayshore Rd.
Palo Alto, CA   94303

Mr Bong L Wong
ESI Engr Services Inc
5135 Port Chicago Hwy
Concord, CA   94520

Mr Richard G Woodard
Terratech Inc
1365 Vander Way
San Jose, CA   95112

Mr Thomas D Wosser
H.J. Degenkolb Associates
350 Sansome St
San Francisco, CA   94104

Dr Sheng-Chi Wu
Bechtel Power Corp.
3226 Ashlock Dr.
Houston, TX   87082

Prof E B Wylie
Univ of Michigan
Dept of Civil Engineering
Ann Arbor, MI   48109

Prof Zhen D Xue

2033 Haste St #102
Berkeley, CA   94704

Mr Rodney K Whitten
USAF Cvl Engr
630 Sansome St Rm 1316
San Francisco, CA   94111

Mr Robert G Wilkinson
Cnty of San Bernardino
825 East Third St
San Bernardino, CA   92415-0832

Edward L Wilson
Univ of Calif
1050 Leneve Pl
El Cerrito, CA   94530

Mr David J Wisch
Texaco USA
P.O. Box 60252
New Orleans, LA   70160

Mr Erwin P Wollak

255 Claremont Blvd.
San Francisco, CA   94127

Dr Julius P Wong
University of Louisville
Mechanical Engineering Dept.
Louisville, KY   40292

Prof Richard D Woods
Univ of Michigan
Rm 2322 G.G. Brown Lab
Ann Arbor, MI   48109

Steve Wright
USAE WES
WES POBx 631
Vicksburg, MS   39180

Spencer Wu
Nat Bureau Standards

Gaitherburg, MD   20899

Mr Loring A Wyllie Jr.
H.J. Degenkolb Assoc.
350 Sansome St # 500
San Francisco, CA   94104

Bojidar S Yanev
TAMS
655 3rd Ave
New York, NY   10017

Prof C. Y Yang
University of Delaware
Civil Engineering Dept.
Newark, DE   19711

Dr Ming-San Yang
NCT Engineering, Inc.
P. O. Box 1937
Lafayette, CA   94549

Hsiang-Jen Yen
Sargent & Lundy
55 E Monroe St
Chicago, IL   60603

Dr Robert K Yin
Cosmos Corporation
1730 K St., N.W. Suite 1302
Washington, D.C.   20006

Dr Manabu Yoshimura
Univ. of California
2365 Hilgard Ave.
Berkeley, CA   94709

Dr Tony F Zahrah
Agbabian Associates
250 N. Nash
El Segundo, CA   90245

Dr X. Zeng
Princeton Univ.
Dept. of Civil Eng. E220 E-Quad
Princeton, NJ   08544

Domenic Zigant
West Div Navfac
Box 727
San Bruno, CA   94010

Dr David S Yang
Assoc. Geotechnical Engineers
1440 Koll Circle, Suite 106
San Jose, CA   95112

Prof James T Yao
Purdue University
School of Civil Eng.
West Lafayette, IN   47907

Dr Solomon C Yim
U.C. Berkeley
410 Davis Hall
Berkeley, CA   94720

Prof Jin Yoshimura
Univ. of California, Berkeley
1412 Spring Way
Berkeley, CA   94708

Dr T. L Youd
USGS
345 Middlefield Road
Menlo Park, CA   94025

Dr Mohammed M Zaman
University of Oklahoma
202 W. Boyd, Room 334
Norman, OK   73019

Mr Christos A Zeris
U.C. Berkeley
2390 Parker St. #8
Berkeley, CA   94704

Prof Theodore C Zsutty
San Jose St. University
1579 Peregrino Way
San Jose, CA   95125

U.S.S.R.

Dr Burgman

Moscow

Dr G.S. Pereselenkov
Gosstaeoy USSP
Pushkinskaya St 26
Moscow   103828

Dr Chanukvadze

Moscow, U.S.S.R.

Dr Richagov

Moscow, U.S.S.R.

Dr Shagihian   Dr Yakubov

Moscow   Moscow

United Kingdom

Mr Michael A Alderson   Mr Edmund D Booth
U.K. Atomic Energy Athy   Ove Arup & Partners
Wigshaw Lane   13 Fitzroy St
Warrington, Cheshire   WA3 4NE   London   WLP 6BQ

Mr Andrew W Coburn   Mr John Colloff
Cambridge Univ   B.N.F. p.l.c.
Martin C.A.U.S. C.U. 6 Chaucer Rd   Risley
Cambridge   CB2 2EB   Warrington, Cheshire   WA3 6AS

Mr Joseph W Day   Mr Christopher J Derham
Central Electricity Generating Board   Rubber Consultants
G.D.C.D., Barnett Way, Barnwood   Brickendonbury, Hertford
Gloucheste, Glouchestershire 9L4 7RS   Herts   SG13 8NL

Dr Alan Eames-Jones   Mr Brian R Ellis
S.D.R.C. Engineering Services Ltd.   Bldg Rsrch Establishment
York House, Stevenage Road   Building Research Station
Hitchin, Herts   SG4 9DY   Garston, Watford   WD2 7JR

Mr Neville R Geary   NO Henaku
British Nuclear Fuels Plc   UST-Ghana
Risey Room 217 Rutherford House   10 Montague Flats Eugene St
Warrington, Cheshire   WA3 6AS   Bristol   B52 8EU

Richard Hughes   Dr R.G. James
IDI London   Cambridge Univ
45 Crescent Lane   Engr Dpt
London   Trumpington St, Cambridge

Mr David E Key   Dr Tidu Maini
CEP Research   Principia Mechanica Ltd
Churchmill House, Oakford Rd.   50 Vineyard Path
Godalming, Surrey   GU85AQ   London   SW 14

Dr John H Mills   Peter Phelan
Allott & Lomax   Principia Mech Ltd
Fairbairn House, Ashton Lane   50 Vineyard Path
Sale, Manchester   M33 1WP   London   SWIG 8ET

Mr Christopher R Sharman   Dr Bryan O Skipp
Allott and Lomax   Soil Mech Ltd
Fairbairn House Ashton Lane   Foundation House E Rd
Sale, Manchester   M33 1WP   Bracknell, Berkshire   RG12 2UZ

Dr Rodney J Stubbs
NIT
Thames House North
London   SWIP 4DJ

Prof Geoffrey B Warburton
Univ. Of Nottingham
Dept Of Mech Eng Univ Of Nottingham
Nottingham   NG7 2RD

Dr Gordon Woo
Principia Mechanica Ltd.
50 Vineyard Path
London, England   SW14 8ET

Venezuela

Prof Alfonso J Malaver
Funvisis
Av Washington #21-44
San Bernardino, Caracas   1110

Jose A Malaver
Funvisis
Av Washington #21-44
San Bernardino, DF   1010

Dr Agustin A Mazzeo

Altamira Decima Trans Quinta Catira
Caracas   1062

Mr Alberto E Olivares
Academia De Ciencias F.M.N.
Av Los Caobos, Qta Marinor
Caracas

Mr William L Quintero
Univ de los Andes
Apartado 476
Merida   5101

West Germany

Dr Hans-Joachim Alheid
Fed Inst for Geosciences
POBx 51 01 53
Hannover 51   D-3000

Mr Ibrahim A Attalla
Kraftwerk Union AG
Berliner St 295
Offenbach   605

Dr Guenter W Borm
Univ of Karlsruhe
Kaiserstrabe 12
Karlsruhe 1   D-7500

Dr Kresimir Delinec
Kraftwerk Union AG
Hammerbacher St 12-14
Erlangen   8520

Dr Rolf Eligehausen
Univ of Stuttgart, W Germany
Dachswaldweg 74
Stuttgart 80   7000

Mr Uwe Hohlsiepe
Ruhr U. Bochum Ins Konst Ing-bau 3
Universitatsstrabe 150
Bochum   4630

Dr Guenter K Hueffmann
GERB-Germany
21 Sylviastreet
Essen   4300

Dr Einar Keintzel
Univ Karlsruhe
7500 Karlsruhe 1
Karlsruhe   6380

Dr Herbert D Klapperich
Tech Univ Berlin
5 Pacelliallee 5
Berlin 33   1000

Mr Wolfgang Kohler
Munchener Ruckversicherung
107 Koeniginstrabe
Munich 40   8000

Prof Eberhard Luz
Univ Stuttgart
Neuer Berg 26
Stuttgart 60   7000

Dr Ruediger Nortmann
Institut fuer Geophysik
c/o Prof Seweryn Duda, Bundesstr 55
Hamburg 13   D-2000

Mr Willi A Sarfeld
Tech Univ Berlin
Strasse D 17 Juni 135 Sekr B5
Berlin 19   1000

Mr Gunther J Schauer
TUEV Stuttgart
Postfach 13 80
Filderstadt   7024

Dr Anselm J Smolka
Munich Reinsurance Comp.
Koeniginstr. 107
Munich 40   D-8000

Dr Martin Steinwachs
NLLB
Stilleweg 2
Hannover 51   D-3000

Dr Herbert Tiedemann
Swiss Reinsurance Co.
5, Stefan-Rotthaler-Str
Moosburg   D-8052

Dr Horst Werkle
Hochtief AG
Bockenheimer Landstr. 24
Frankfurt   D-6000

Dr Horst P Wolfel
Wolfel Consulting Engineers
Oho-hahn-Strabe 2a
Hochberg   8706

Prof Gunter K Klein
PreuBenelektra AG
Tresckowstrabe 5
Hannover 91   3000

Mr Dieter Konietschke
TUV Bayern e V
Westendstr 199
Munich 21   8000

Prof Otfried P Natau
University of Karlsruhe
5 Stettiner-Strabe
Karlsruhe 1   D-7500

Dr Werner F Ruecker
BAM-Berlin
Unter den Eichen 87
Berlin   D-1000

Dr Otto H Schad
Kraftwerk Union AG
Berliner Strabe 299
Offenbach   6050

Prof Gunther Schmid
Ruhr-Universitat Bochum
Postfach 102148
Bochum 1   D-4630

Dr Friedhelm Stangenberg
Zerna, Schnellenbach & **Partners**
47 Viktoriastrasse
Bochum 1   D-4630

Mr Shengwei Tang
Konig & Heunisch
C/O I.F.M. Alexander **Strabe 5**
Darmstadt   6100

Dr Gunter Waas
Hochtief AG
Bockenheimer Landstr. 24
Frankfurt   D-6000

Dr. Armin O Winkler
GERB Germany
21 Sylvia Street
Essen 1   4300

Johann D Worner
Konig & Heunisch
Letzter Hasenpfad 21
Frankfurt   D 6000

West Indies

Dr. P. Arumugasaamy
Lee Young & Partners
Appt. #2, g Third St., Maraval
Port of Spain, Trinidad

Mr Anthony C Farrell
CEP Ltd
1A Bergerac Rd Maraval POBx 3065
St James, Trinidad

Ms Cheryl-Ann Peters
Lee Young & Partners
Lot #4 William St., Four Roads
Diego Martin, Trinidad

Mr Kristendath Ramkissoon
Lee Young & Partners
14-16 Dere Street
Port of Spain, Trinidad

Mr Philip T Sobers
Consulting Engrs Partnership Ltd
#80 Oxnard 5
St. James, Barbados

Yugoslavia

Dr Nenad Bicanic
Univ of Zagreb, Yugoslavia
Janka Rakuse 1
Zagreb   41000

Prof Peter Fajfar
Univ E Kardelj in Ljubljana
Jamova 2
Ljubljana   61000

Mr Matej Fischinger
Univ E Kardelj in Ljubljana
Jamova 2
Ljubljana   61000

Mr. Dimitar V Jurukovski
I.E.E.S.
Pat Skopje-Vokno b.b. P.O. Box 101
Skopje   91000

Slobodan Kojic
Energoprojekt
Bulevar Lenjina 12
Belgrade   11000

Dr Josko Ozbolt
Gradjevinski Inst
J Rakuse 1 Zagreb
Zagreb   41000

Bozidar Pavicevic
Inst Urban Plan and Design
2 Bulevar Revolucije
Titograd   81000

Zivota Perisic
Fac of Cvl Engr
73 Bulevar Revolucije
Belgrade   11000

Jakim T Petrovski
I.E.E.S.
Pat Skopje-Vodno b.b. P.O. Box 101
Skopje   91000

Mr Peter F Sheppard
Inst for Tst & Rsrch Mat & Stru ZRMK
Dimiceva 12
Ljubljana   61000

Boris Simeonov
Ins of E-Quake And Engr Seis
Pat Skopje Vodno 66 POBx101
Skopje   91000

Vucic Slobodan
Gro Rad Dsgn Office
31 Kosovska PO Bx 9
Belgrade   11000

Mr Miha Tomazevic
Ins for Tst & Rsrch Mat & Structs
Dimiceva 12
Ljubljana   61000

Paskalov Trifun
Ins E-Quake Engr and Seismology
Pat Skopje-Yodno 66 POB   101
Skopje   91000

Prof Andrej Umek
Univ of Maribor
Smetanova 17
Maribor   62000

Mr Roko Zarnic
Ins for Tst & Rsrch Mat & Strucs
Dimiceva 12
Ljubljana   61000

Prof Miodrag P Velkov
I.E.E.E.S.
Pat Skopje-Vodno b.b. P.O. Box 101
Skopje   91 000

Others

Ben H Hallou
Algeria

Dr. William D Kovacs
Nat Bureau of Standards
Washington, D.C.

Marv L McCauley

Luciano Nunziante

Ben Schmid

Shigeru Suzuki
Stanford

VIII. ERRATA FOR THE FIRST SEVEN VOLUMES

VOLUME IV, Page 451.

The paper "Possible Extensions of the Structural Seismic Analysis" by D. Capatina and Em. Titaru was printed with incorrect order of pages. The correct order of the pages is 451, 452, 455, 456, 453, 454, 457, 458.

The Proceedings Committee apologizes to the authors and readers for this error.